P9-CEP-261

BACHELOR
PARTY
CONFIDENTIAL

BACHELOR PARTY CONFIDENTIAL

A Real-Life Peek Behind the Closed-Door Tradition

DAVID BOYER

SSE SIMON SPOTLIGHT ENTERTAINMENT
Simon & Schuster, New York

NEW YORK LONDON TORONTO SYDNEY

SIMON SPOTLIGHT ENTERTAINMENT

An imprint of Simon & Schuster

1230 Avenue of the Americas, New York, New York 10020

Text copyright © 2007 by David Boyer

All rights reserved, including the right of reproduction

in whole or in part in any form.

SIMON SPOTLIGHT ENTERTAINMENT and related logo

are trademarks of Simon & Schuster, Inc.

Manufactured in the United States of America

First Edition 2 4 6 8 10 9 7 5 3 1

Library of Congress Control Number 2006028399

ISBN-13: 978-1-4169-2808-9

ISBN-10: 1-4169-2808-1

"Come on in! Drugs to the right, hookers to the left."

—*Bachelor Party* (1984)

Contents

NOTE TO THE READER:

Names and locations have been changed to protect the innocent (and not so innocent).

Why Me?

WHORES, BOOZE, AND TRASHED HOTEL ROOMS. TRANS-
vestite strippers, vengeful brides, and a battalion of cops. Like
most kids who came of age during the Reagan years, that's how I
assumed men celebrated the night before their wedding, thanks
to that mildly raunchy Tom Hanks vehicle *Bachelor Party*.

When I finally attended one—my older cousin's in 1988—
the movie's influence was hard to miss: The party was a deca-
dent swirl of chugging, drugging, backslapping, and taunting
at a rent-for-the-evening Tribeca loft tricked out with black
leather couches and lots of neon. The pot was imported from
Maui, the "lesbian" strippers from New Jersey. I had seen my
cousin and his friends get messy plenty of times, but this night
into morning was different: They seemed desperate to make a
statement. But about what?

I didn't stick around to find out. High as a kite, I excused myself when the floor show led to a free-for-all, during which my cousin's fraternity pals took turns inserting a glass soda bottle into the talent's nether regions. Truth be told, I was closeted back then. And while I was scandalized by the bottle trick, I was more worried that my actions at the party—or lack thereof—would betray my secret.

So how and why does a gay guy end up writing a book about bachelor parties?

I've always been fascinated by traditions and the revelatory ways different people mark the same occasion. The follow-up to my first book—which was about queers and the prom—was supposed to be a kitsch-free look at bar mitzvah traditions around the world. That changed one night at a cocktail party when a friend asked, "What's next? Bachelor parties?" We both laughed—and then I jotted it down in my Treo.

A few days later I headed to the New York Public Library. Out of the more than twenty million books in its collection— most no longer in print—there was only one dedicated exclusively to the ritual: a how-to guide, courtesy of *Playboy*.

Why hadn't somebody already written this book? Then it hit me: Like joining a fraternity, a man's participation in a bachelor party is contingent on sworn secrecy and reservation of judgments. Thus, a straight guy writing a book about what really goes on would be akin to treason. And women, well, they're not on the guest list. Perhaps it would take a gay man to get to the heart of the most hetero of hetero traditions.

Any hesitation about spending a couple of years in Guyville

was exorcised by what I took as a sign: an invitation to the bachelor party of a close friend from college. How could I say no?

So there we were—two dozen straight guys from across the country, and me—whooping it up at a lake house in the Sierras. For four exhaustingly carefree days, we ate, drank, cooked, played, inhaled, snorted, and snored together amid the fifty-inch glow of round-the-clock porn. This was a much more enlightened and organized group than my cousin's posse. In fact, the theme of the main event was "Captain's Happy Hour," with everyone in attendance dressed homoerotically in matching sailor suits, including a petite blond stripper.

I was floored when I found out how much they spent to procure her: one thousand dollars for a couple of hours (my share: a reasonable fifty bucks). Once she shed her captain's hat and panties, I understood what all the fuss what about: All eyes were on her vagina; it was as if these guys had never seen one before. For the first time in days, they were largely speechless.

The rest of the weekend, on the other hand, I felt especially connected to these men, who, in many cases, I've known for more than a decade. Career plans, sexual adventures, spiritual awakenings, fucked-up childhoods, pregnant wives— everything was discussed. "Good, clean male bonding," I scribbled in my journal as I flew back to New York City. "Fun, flirty, macho, sexy bonding."

The all-guys weekend was unexpectedly moving, maybe because it doesn't happen that often. While exclusively male gatherings were once the norm, these days men rarely assemble without girlfriends, wives, or female coworkers and friends.

The only time we hear or read about male-only get-togethers is when something goes drastically wrong (like the Duke lacrosse scandal) or when women are trying to gain admission (men's golf and Annapolis). And as pressure mounts from brides, girl-friends, families, and the media to sanitize the bachelor party and/or include women, the time is right to explore one of the last bastions of male bonding.

As I told a stripper who I interviewed early on, I don't have a horse in this race. My agenda is not to protect my brothers nor ruin their fun. I simply hope to present different expres-sions of a rite of passage that crosses cultural, generational, and geographic lines. In a culture obsessed with celebrity, I set out to hear from everyday people from all walks of life. I wanted to know what the ritual meant to each of them, how it's affected their relationships, and how it's changed over the years.

And that's exactly what I did.

I talked with more than one hundred men from around the country and all over the globe—men from different generations, classes, and backgrounds. I also chatted with, among others, two strippers, a dwarf, an S&M clown, a Vegas bouncer, and a pair of wedding planners. I spoke with reli-gious grooms, wary brides, and the fathers who love them. I interviewed guys who prefer to skip the festivities altogether, and guys who never miss the opportunity.

I offered total anonymity to everyone I approached. In return they served up a grab bag of painful, poignant, secret, and salacious stories—stories I sensed that many had been dying to tell for years.

Their personal anecdotes provide a revealing portrait of a ritual that, at first blush, seems at odds with the institution of marriage. At a time when men are pigeonholed as either metrosexuals or Neanderthals, this is a candid and varied look at what's going on inside their minds. And, for the first time, it is also an uncensored look at what they do when women aren't around.

So find a comfy chair, pour yourself a drink, and prepare, as they say in the wedding biz, for better or for worse.

THE HAPPY COUPLE
Andy W. & Allyson W.

Andy W., a financial expert, and Allyson W., a fashion executive, were kind enough to talk—separately and anonymously—about Andy's bachelor party in 1991, and subsequent bachelor parties for "the Boys," his close-knit group of friends from junior high and high school. "They're a really good group of guys," says Allyson, mother of three, from her home in Atlanta. "If I had to pick a group of friends for my husband, this would be the group that I would pick."

Andy: I was one of the first to get married. My bachelor party was okay. I was living in Florida, so all the Boys flew down, and my brother took care of the arrangements.

Allyson: I tried not to think about it, because you hear that the groom has sex or there are blow jobs, and everybody gets drunk. You know, it's this wild and crazy time, because the groom thinks, "Oh, this is my last opportunity to be with somebody, or to do things a single person would do." That was—and I guess still is— my impression of bachelor parties.

Andy: My bachelor party met my expectations, because I didn't know any better. But it was sterile, because there was no extracurricular activity or what I call "side jobs." It was basically hot-oil wrestling in a ring, and there were two girls wearing little shorts. And my brother got to rub the oil on them and prepare them to wrestle me. And there's a guy who moderates and makes a bunch of stupid and funny

CHAPTER 1

He Said, She Said

THERE ARE AT LEAST TWO SIDES TO EVERY STORY. But when it comes to bachelor parties, there are more like twenty. There's the best man's version, the entertainment's, the attendees', and the innocent bystanders'. All have a unique vantage point and something specific to contribute to the full picture. And in time we'll hear from all of them.

To start, however, let's focus on the happy couple. Unless the wedding guest list is heavy on the exes, the bachelor party is probably the pair's last big test before they walk down the aisle, with the groom caught between friends ready for debauchery and a skittish bride who, whether she'll admit it or not, is worried he'll be tempted to cheat. How husband and wife think about the bachelor party (and negotiate the ground rules) is a pretty good indicator of what's in store after they say, "I do."

comments and shit. They videotape it and give you the tape at the end of the night. That was probably the only thing that made it so cool: that I got to see it after. I brought it home and showed it to my wife the night before we left for our honeymoon.

Allyson: Our wedding was late morning/early afternoon. By early evening it was over. And we get into the limo, and Andrew was extremely upset because apparently he specifically requested a car with a VCR so he could show me his bachelor party video. I, on the other hand, was really not so upset because, quite frankly, I was not interested in watching my husband with another woman the night of my wedding.

When we checked into the hotel, he made sure that we had a VCR. So we get to the room, and he puts in the video. The whole time I'm telling him, "You know what, I really don't want to watch this." If he sensed my unease, I don't really think he cared; he was so excited about it that he wanted me to see it. But the timing sucked. Are you kidding me? It was horrible; it was almost like watching your husband in a soft-core porn movie.

I guess it does make me feel good that he wanted to show it to me, because it kinda means that he feels close enough that he could share something so personal that didn't include me. I don't remember feeling jealous when I watched. That's one good thing about our relationship: There is like, 100 percent trust . . . at least on my side. So it's not that, you know, every time he goes out I'm worried. I mean there have been times—I can't believe I'm telling you this—that Andy and I would be driving down the street with our kids. And this car pulls up with these young girls. And he'll say, "Put your head down, put your head down, I have to look at these girls."

And I'm like, "Are you crazy? You're a guy driving a minivan with three kids in the backseat. Do you really think they're gonna look at you?" That's kind of the relationship that we have. I think it's all in fun. Of course, it could be a ploy to throw me off, but I guess because a lot of it is in front of me, I don't really worry about it.

Andy: After my party, she came up with the "Rules" for future bachelor parties: There's no kissing; there's no licking. There's no touching of wet parts—that would be a vagina. And no sniffing—you know, smelling a girl's vagina.

Wives need to be realistic. I find it unrealistic to have a wife say, "I don't want you going near vagina. I don't want you touching boobs. I don't want anybody stripping in front of you." I don't think that's right. My wife has a great sense of humor: no touching of wet parts. Okay, I can't stick my finger in some girl's vagina.

Allyson: My husband is extremely sexual. Obviously I think he is a very handsome man. He also has the ability to make anybody that he's with feel special and good about themselves. You know, he's a charmer. And I know sexually what he likes and what he wants. Some guys are boob guys, some guys are ass guys. Andrew is all about the bottom half of the body: the wet parts.

I was never upset that he was going to bachelor parties, but the Rules were just so that he knew that this is where I was coming from, and that this is what I didn't want to happen. So, however he was able to maneuver around those rules was up to him, I guess.

For my bachelorette party, all I wanted to do was go out to dinner with friends. That's it. Going to clubs, having a guy do whatever, that doesn't interest me; I'd rather be with my husband. But the guys were always really excited about the bachelor parties. They probably felt that they could do whatever they wanted and there was nobody there to get mad at them or say you can't do this or that. It's like a rite of passage for them. And it's probably something that most men feel they need to experience to one degree or another. All right, so be it. So long as it stops there.

Andy: I guess for some guys the bachelor party is about turning yourself into a real man and becoming a real husband and going into a long-term, monogamous relationship, and saying goodbye to all the bullshit. But my friends are not very philosophical. We want to see pussy. I don't think it is anything deeper.

While I wasn't able to do that at my party, as the rest of the Boys got married, the bachelor parties all got greater and greater. I'm telling you, the third and the fourth and the fifth, those were the real good, juicy, disgusting ones.

After me, the next guy to get engaged was Jimmy P. And I'm like, "I will be in charge of doing the bachelor party." So me and one of the other Boys got together and found a lady named Josie.

Josie would bring over a binder of pictures of girls, and basically I would go thumb through it. You know, it was kind of a funny thing, but it was very cool. We always wanted one hot girl and one girl for degradation, which is disgusting to say, being a forty-year-old, and I have three daughters; just so you know, I believe God is getting back at me for what I have done—not just at bachelor parties.

So yeah, one's for degradation and that was Crazy Mary's forte. Back in the nineties, they did not have, or I did not hire, what they have now; nowadays they can pop shit out of their vaginas or puff a cigar. Back in my day, it was a ketchup-bottle-insertion program; it was a tall beer bottle. And Crazy Mary was a perennial. At every party we had, she was in attendance; we pretty much had her ass on retainer.

I'm sure most guys kept a lot of shit close to their chest. But if you ask my wife about Crazy Mary, she'd say, "Oh yeah, she's the girl who goes to all the parties and would take bottles and, you know, do disgusting stuff."

I didn't do side jobs. I think you gotta know before you get married that you're going in for the long haul—with this piece of ass for the rest of your life.

Allyson: I know about the two strippers: One is usually pretty and one will do whatever they want. But other than that, I don't really know. I don't know who did what. I don't know if anything was done. One of his friends did allude to the fact that things definitely happen at those bachelor parties. But he wouldn't say anything else. So it's still kind of a secret.

Andy: Josie would always also bring a few extra girls. You would go to the bathroom and get oral; you would go to the bathroom and get a hand job. I don't think any of the Boys availed themselves of that, but a lot of the other guys at the party definitely did. You know, we all went away to college at different places, so we all made friends that would be involved in the bachelor parties. And it was the imported guys that typically went for the side jobs.

The third party I think was Dave's. And he got so drunk so fast that he passed out at the party. Before he passed out, Dave kept saying, "My uncle's here," and he felt kind of squeamish about that. So we immediately sent Crazy Mary to play with Dave's Uncle Herb and to put him in a compromising position; she sat with him and pushed her boobies in his uncle's face, whatever. But this way, Uncle Herb would keep his mouth shut and wouldn't go back to Dave's father and say, "Hey, you should have seen what they did at the party."

But really Dave could not avail himself of anything, because he passed out so early in the party. So that was a lesson for the next party.

Each of the parties got progressively better. The last one was for Swish; it was at a private club that really did not have that much privacy. Of course we had the veteran Mary, who at this time, the joke is, was retired in Florida and we had to pull her out of retirement. We also had a lot of side jobs.

I didn't do side jobs. I think you gotta know before you get married that you're going in for the long haul—with this piece of ass for the rest of your life. And if you can't come to terms with it, don't get married.

Allyson: I don't know if he did or he didn't; he didn't tell me if he did. But I think that if you're getting married to somebody, you need to trust that person. And that person needs to respect you enough to honor that trust. And I think if you're going into a marriage thinking your husband is going to have sex at a bachelor party, maybe you should rethink what you are doing.

Andy: Most men are *not* going to cheat at the bachelor party, because all your guys are there. Even if you do have side jobs in the bathroom or wherever, you know who's going back there. I know who went back there. But *I* would *never* fucking tell anybody.

Infamous Bachelor Parties:
SEAN SULLIVAN, 2004

Their comeback was cemented with a very public walk down the aisle, but former Newlyweds **Jessica Simpson** and **Nick Lachey** hit a snag after tabloids claimed that Nick was getting a little grabby with porn star **Jessica Jaymes**, who was performing at Sullivan's bachelor party in the Hollywood Hills. While all concerned denied that anything untoward occurred at the time, the pop pair split two years later.

THE SOON-TO-BE BRIDE
Wendy K.

Wendy K. wasn't particularly worried about her fiancé cheating the day after he left for his five-day bachelor party in South Beach. "I don't feel nervous, even though you always hear these crazy stories," explains the pretty, petite twenty-four-year-old, who lives in New Jersey. "To be honest, I've told him, 'Go ahead! See if there is somebody better out there. You can try.' But trust me, no one else is going to put up with him. And he's not stupid enough to make that kind of mistake anyway, whether he's on a bachelor party or out with the guys here." Besides, Wendy, an office manager and natural-born organizer, had something more important on her mind: her bachelorette party.

I don't really care about his party—does that sound mean? I'm just looking forward to mine. One group of friends has planned something for Friday night that is completely a surprise. For Saturday, which is my official bachelorette party, the plan is to go in the morning and get tattoos; I'm an angel fanatic and I am definitely leaning toward getting angel wings on the top of my foot—although my mother's advice was to put it someplace dirty, so you can let the hair grow back in if you don't like it. (She is *so* bad!)

My fiancé doesn't know; he is going to die when he finds out. He kind of has this preconceived notion: It's good for the guys to look at the girls that have the tattoos, but his own woman shouldn't have one, because it's trashy. Whatever. I'm not killing somebody. And I've always wanted to get a tattoo, but was too scared to do it. This just gives me a little extra incentive to go for it. Because once you do get married, then you start wanting to plan a family. And people look at you differently, so you have to do things differently.

After getting tattoos, we're going to brunch and to get manicures and pedicures. Then we are going out to dinner in the city. As a little surprise gift for my girls, I'm getting two little people[1] to meet us at my house in Jersey an hour before the limo comes to take us to dinner. One is a woman and one is a guy, and they're coming dressed as gangsters. They're going to greet all my guests, do a mini striptease, wrestle in a kiddie pool of Jell-O, and then we are going to take pictures. They're also going to serve drinks and give my guests little appetizers. How great is that? I've always loved little people; I don't know why. I guess it's humorous. And with a regular stripper, some people might feel embarrassed, but if you go with a little person, it's just more like a joke; it's entertaining and everyone can feel comfortable and not be shy.

I am planning on purposely getting trashed so I can sleep all day Sunday. We do have plans for all the girls to sleep over at my place; we're going to have a big slumber party. I have four married women coming who have been married for like twenty or thirty years—they're just looking forward to a nice, peaceful evening away from their husbands.

A lot of people say the bachelorette party is your last night out. But that's a load of crap. My reason for doing it is more social, to get together with everyone that is really close to me, because we're always too busy to get together; if it's once a month, we feel lucky.

....

1 little people (n) aka midgets and dwarfs

This is one night where everybody can just go out, relax, have a few drinks, laugh, enjoy the company, and then go back to the normal everyday routine.

I actually went to a bachelorette party last week. We just went out to dinner and to a nightclub and then a strip club. It was nice; we touched some guy's ass. But we did have one girl that is engaged who actually met somebody in the nightclub and took him back to the limo, did the nasty, and came back. Swear to God: She is getting married in September. And I was like, "I cannot believe it." We were all shocked. Like, "That's not right; someone should tell her fiancé." She actually told him today—and he kind of forgave her. You know, the wedding is still on. Guys are dirty, but girls can be just as dirty.

So, how do you think your party will differ from your fiancé's?

I don't know. I'm sure they're hanging out on the beach and drinking. And they'll go out to the social clubs at night. But God knows what they'll do; I know they do the topless-bar thing. If he feels the need to give a chick extra money, that's fine. Not four hundred dollars extra, but if he wants to give her a few singles—to each his own. I always tell him, "I got the same shit, just a different size." But I think it's like a macho thing for them; they're just trying to act cool when all the guys are together.

There are no rules. All I simply said was, "Be careful. Have a good time. Don't do anything stupid." And I told him he didn't have to call me while he was away. You know, "Call me when you land and when you're ready to leave." But he's been calling me, so . . . I just want him to get the full feeling and actually enjoy the guys' weekend.

I don't know if I'll talk to him on Saturday, because it's kind of going to be my day—just for me and the girls. I can't wait. I'm so excited!

I checked in with Wendy a few days after her party. She didn't end up getting that tattoo after the doctor she works for scared her with a laundry list of dangers and detractions. Instead she surprised her hubby-to-be by buying a new Mercedes. He, on the other hand, returned a day early from his bachelor getaway because, according to Wendy, he and his buddies were having a hard time getting into the clubs.

THE UNDERCOVER BRIDE
Melissa D.

Some brides want to know everything that happened at the groom's bachelor party, but there's definitely an argument to be made for staying in the dark. Los Angeles–based writer Melissa D., who likes to say she is "older than Britney Spears and younger than Demi Moore," learned that lesson when she went undercover at her fiancé's party for a women's magazine.

My editors at the magazine knew I was getting married. And they called and asked, "Is your husband having a bachelor party? And would you crash it as a man?" I was like, *"Of course!* I wanna know what's happening." I think all girls do. And as a journalist, I was like, "Well, I'm getting paid," and I was a struggling freelancer at that time.

I went to the magazine's office, and this makeup artist made me up as a man with a little mustache. And a stylist put me in these clothes, a brown shirt and these ugly pants with pleats. It was fine, but I looked so bad; I looked like this little fat Chinese man.

My brother was my partner in crime: He was throwing the party and he told me where it was going to be and all that. And he had to tell everybody (except my fiancé) what was going on, because otherwise there might be problems. Nobody squealed. And because there were photographers for the story, my brother told my fiancé, Mike, it was for a coffee-table book on bachelor parties, and Mike was like, "All right, whatever. Just don't use my name."

I caught up with the party at a strip club. Actually, I was surprised that the girls there were very pretty: They didn't have fake boobs, they were young, and kind of gorgeous. And I was like, "Oh, shit!" because I was expecting some over-tanned, forty-year-old, sagging, over-the-hill strippers. But no, they were nubile college girls.

The place, though, was kind of sleazy. Very dark; all these corner booths. There was a lone stage in the middle, where somebody would dance. And because I was there dressed as a man, the strippers would come up to me, like, "You want a dance?" They wanted to give me a lap dance. And I'd be like, "No, no." But they were very aggressive. What's funny is I had to go to the bathroom—and I was *not* gonna go to the men's room—so I tried to go in the women's bathroom. And the strippers were like, "You're not allowed!" I confessed, "I'm a girl!" and explained that I was a journalist. Well, the women's bathroom is also the strippers' dressing room. And they had this great camaraderie in there, and they were really cool.

My brother and the rest of the party were already there when I arrived. I watched as the girls hopped on and off my fiancé's lap and slithered up against his belly, stuck his face between their breasts, and bent over to give him a better view of their backsides. Seeing him enjoy himself was a little bit, uh, troubling.

For some reason, I thought he would be bored—I guess because I would be bored. But no, he had a smile on his face and this wolflike grin. You never want to think of your husband as somebody who looks at other women. And I didn't think all these very educated, liberal, feminist men were gonna have that much fun. They're not like typical jock guys; they're art history majors and writers and architects. I mean, Mike originally said he didn't really want a bachelor party or need one. He thinks they're just silly. He always says, "It's like the most unsexy thing. It's all fake. You're flirting with a stripper, and of course she laughs at your jokes." Yeah. *Whatever!* These are just lies men tell women to make us feel better. [*laughs*] What I learned is that even if your husband's very enlightened, at heart, he's very male. They do like seeing the boobs. And here's this place where it's totally allowed and expected and encouraged.

I did feel kind of bad because I was spying. You know, some things should be private. But they had their little private thing afterward; they went to another strip club after I left. I really didn't need to see any more. I've never heard about what happened later; I'm sure it was nothing. I think they just wanted to enjoy that whole "last night of freedom." But really his last night of freedom was the night before he met me.

At one point, Mike walked right by me. We made eye contact, but there was no recognition whatsoever. That was really freaky, 'cause I felt like, "I'm here!" We'd been dating for six years; I thought he would just mentally recognize me, but he totally didn't. I don't know what I would have done if he did: I would've just been like, "It's just for a magazine." Ha ha, funny! Your bachelor party's a part of my career. I would have just confessed and tried to laugh it off; I knew he would have probably understood.

They just wanted to enjoy that whole "last night of freedom." But really his last night of freedom was the night before he met me.

I told him a week later. We were at dinner somewhere kind of nice. And after several glasses of wine, I was like, "You know that bachelor party you had?" He was like, "Uh-huh." I was like, "Well, there was a weird Chinese guy in the back; that was me." And he totally remembered. He was like, "You were the weird, creepy Chinese guy in the corner? I'm gonna kill you!" But he was fine with it. He thought it was hilarious. And we were definitely very happy when we got the check for the article, because we needed the money.

I was afraid when the article came out that there'd be some negative blowback, but people really liked it; I think it touched upon something women are very curious about. And people definitely wanted to know whether we were still getting married. So, in the next issue it said, "Mike and Melissa got married. They're fine."

So many of my friends who were getting married called me and were like, "Oh my God, I totally want to do what you did!" I think girls are worried. But the bachelor party is not really about love and it's not really about your wedding—it's just about having fun with the boys. And boys will be boys. So I was like, "Don't do it. Do you really want that image seared in your brain—some woman's butt in your husband's face?"

Melissa didn't realize until very recently what actually occurs when the strippers give a lap dance: "They're really grinding their butt on your soon-to-be-husband's you-know-what. And I was always the cool chick. We would go to Vegas and topless bars, and I'd buy him lap dances; I think I was just in denial." And now that she knows? "When I found out, I was like, 'That'll never happen again.' But I don't know how I feel about it. Sleeping with the stripper and getting a hand job, that's not cool—that's crossing the line. But watching naked girls is okay. You know, you can't be *that* uptight."

Virtual Debate
Men and Women Discuss the Ritual

The anonymity of the Internet works like truth serum. Strangers connect, sharing their darkest secrets, their biggest fears, and most incendiary opinions. That's precisely what I found in a bachelor party thread on LoveShack.org, a coed relationship website: men and women talking frankly about the party, the strippers, and the definition of "cheating."

SUBJECT: He Cheated at His BP

InstantKharma: I got married about two months ago. After a lot of prior discussion, my husband decided he wanted to go to a strip club for his bachelor party. We were going through couples' counseling at the time, so one of our sessions before we got married was centered around the ground rules. Basically what was agreed was that he was allowed to go to a topless bar; no private dances or lap dances. I even sent my father along to make sure things wouldn't get TOO out of control.

Flash to that night: all my fiancé's friends came home completely trashed—one even urinated on himself on my couch. I asked if anything got out of control, and everyone told me that my husband was a really good boy.

Two days before the wedding, however, my husband decided to come clean. It was a full-nude bar. The best man had paid for a private "dance" for my husband alone in a room. After a lot of crying, grilling, sobbing, and talking, my husband swore to me the girl never touched him and he never touched her.

Then, on the honeymoon, I kept finding out more and more. Apparently my father had picked the sleaziest place in the area to bring all the boys to. Apparently my father frequents this place, and my *father* and other members of my family also got lap dances. Apparently the girl was very nude and had every intention of giving my husband a lap dance. He swore he told her no, he felt bad for going there, and nothing else happened.

I knew something else went on; it just didn't make sense. I confronted him, and he confessed that the girl was paid to let him do whatever he wanted to her, and he did.

My husband ended up touching her A LOT, including manually having sex with her (using his fingers). He swears this is all that happened, but now I can't help but believe there may be more. I hate myself for still being in this house, and I especially hate him for ruining such a sacred event in my life.

Supermom: I am so sorry to hear about this! I would either go to marriage counseling or get your marriage annulled. How dare he? And maybe you should go on a solo trip out of town . . . let him worry for once.

thatjustsucks: I have heard so many bad stories about bachelor parties and strippers—I know of three marriages that almost split up because of them. And yet people still do it. I would get the annulment. He ruined your honeymoon

He Said, She Said

and the initial gaga world that comes with the first year of marriage. Show him you are serious. You can always marry him again . . . if he proves himself to you.

Wellnowuknow: OMG it was a bachelor party!! He had to get his one more time before he was tied down for the rest of his life! Get over it. He married you, not the stripper—that's all that matters.

BadassBob: Maybe the bachelor party was an unconscious manifestation of his desire to sabotage the relationship . . . a last-ditch effort to escape your stranglehold over him.

Oh, and don't all you ladies jump on the "he's a bum, run away as fast as you can" bandwagon. If this relationship was as rock solid as it should have been to justify getting married, there's NO way the groom-in-waiting would have done anything to jeopardize his future with his bride-to-be. Period.

MrsPinky: I CRIED reading your post, Kharma, mainly because I'd had a similar thing happen to me. I couldn't help but feel like there was something wrong with me, because in a way I felt like he had chosen HER over me.

VancouverGuy: Inserting a finger in a stripper is not cheating (well, not *really* cheating). It was his stag, he was drinking, it was his last chance with a strange piece of . . .

Would I be pissed if my ex-fiancée jerked a guy off at a

strip joint? Yes, but I don't consider it cheating. Besides, strip clubs are very strict about not letting you touch the strippers—some will let you touch their breasts, but not many.

leesgirl: When Vancouver is married and his wife comes home and says, "But a bj isn't REALLY cheating," he'll understand. Men like him are where the phrase "Men are dogs" comes from.

Ladies, it seems we have to spell out every little thing at the beginning of a relationship to make sure it's understood exactly what cheating is to us. Vancouver should give you a heads-up that some men think only vaginal sex is cheating.

BuilderWife: Strippers are nasty skanks who get absolutely no attention with their clothes on. They strip for drunk men so they can get an occasional compliment. They have no class. Otherwise they'd be working a normal job.

JohnJohn: Not all strippers are nasty skanks. Please don't stereotype strippers. A lot of them are just trying to get by, feed their kids, and make a living. Nowadays, a regular-paying job unfortunately doesn't pay all the bills.

For my bachelor party, I went to an all-nude strip club. My brother bought me a VIP dance. All she did was bring me into this little room, put a song on, and laid me on the couch. She took off her shirt, kept her G-string on, and fondled her boobs some. Then she lay on top of me and nuzzled my neck. She told me she's been doing it for ten years and she has no trust in men. It's not the dancer's fault that these guys have sex with them. These dancers don't owe any of you women anything. Yes, it's morally wrong, but it takes two to tango. If your guy wants to cheat, he'll cheat no matter what. You can't stop him from [giving in to] every single temptation. That's more like being a parent than a wife.

In my case, if the dancer wanted to do more or kiss me, I would have stopped her. Most dancers won't do anything unless the guy asks for it, and usually he has to pay up-front.

BuilderWife: You're a MAN! Of course you don't think strippers are skanks. But was she pretty? Was she prettier than your wife? Would you rather have her grinding you than your wife? Are her boobs better than your wife's? These are the questions we jealous wives want answered.

JohnJohn: Yes, she was pretty. No, she was not prettier than my wife. I would rather my wife grind on me than the other chick. Boobs? I prefer my wife's. But it really doesn't matter. If this dancer was ten times better looking than my wife, I still love my wife with all of my heart and would not do anything with this dancer. You are assuming that just because a dancer is better looking than a guy's wife, he's going to sleep with her. That's not true. Men do have brains, and we can use them.

MrSpock: What he TELLS you happened does not cover half. If he was smart, he didn't f*ck her. But she probably gave him head, if he wasn't too drunk to get it up. If he confesses to touching her, it's as good as f*cking her.

ClayMate: I am a male and I would certainly never go to a strip club for my bachelor party, but I know that whoever marries me will be allowed to do whatever the heck she wants for her bachelorette party as long as it isn't sexual contact. How can I be so cavalier? Because only a woman I TRUST will wear my wedding ring.

THE ENLIGHTENED BACHELOR
Gregory C.

Brides are clearly having an influence on the bachelor party, and many aren't afraid to voice their disapproval of including strippers. "Fifty years ago, a woman may have thought the same thing, but had no opportunity to say anything. If she had, it would have been fair for her fiancé to say, 'We are not going to discuss it—the conversation is closed,'" says Gregory C. This dapper Chicago newlywed had a co-ed bachelor party with his wife-to-be after his bachelor party plans became an unexpected point of contention. "Women have a lot more voice in relationships now," he adds. "Therefore, it gives men more of a challenge, but also a *true* partner."

I wanted to go to a shooting range. I thought about going out to a casino. As it turned out, the guys I was inviting weren't into traveling too far and the whole gun thing wasn't attractive to most of them, so we dropped those ideas.

Then we started thinking about something more traditional. I had never been to a traditional bachelor party, and I wanted to see what it is all about. If this is the way to "really party," then, well, I like to party! And who doesn't like to get drunk with their friends and have a good time?

No matter how much I enjoy hanging out with women—because I do very much—when you are with a bunch of guys, the whole atmosphere is different. For instance, when we bought our engagement and wedding rings, my fiancée and I did it together—like we do most things. We found a guy who was very old-school European. He was an excellent salesman, and he complimented us incessantly about how beautiful we were as a couple, how we would have a beautiful marriage, and how he hoped we would have many beautiful children.

We saw him two or three times together, and before the wedding I went to pick up the wedding rings by myself. Instead of wishing me luck on our wedding or talking to me, man-to-man, about what qualities a good husband should possess, he wondered if I was having a bachelor party. And he regaled me with stories of friends and former clients who had had bachelor parties. He got down to the nitty-gritty details about prostitutes and blow jobs. He went from being very PG to being X rated; one minute he was Disney, the next minute he was San Fernando Valley.

My best man and I never actually planned anything that involved the "traditional" bachelor party themes. Before I made any plans, my fiancée and I got to talking. And I mentioned, very naively, "I don't know what we'll do, but maybe there'll be a stripper." And her eyebrows arched, and she said, "Really? Do you want that?" I thought, *Do I?* I wanted the *option*.

My wife is definitely a feminist. And she is a social worker. At one point in our conversation, she said, "These women, they could be my clients." At that time she was working with low-income women; some of them were stripping, and they were all struggling to get by in typically abusive relationships with men. And she sees the sex industry as continually recycling these notions of male power more than female power or empowerment. She sees it as a negative thing, and I feel similarly. However, for my own enjoyment, perhaps I was tempted to nudge my own moral judgments aside for a few moments and take a peek. I saw it as maybe this once-in-a-lifetime thing. And I found it frustrating that there was no counterargument other than, "I want to behave like a juvenile guy. I want to be a boy—and this is what boys do. They want to go see tits." That argument didn't really measure up.

At first, when she said she was uncomfortable with my feelings and surprised that I even was considering having strippers, I felt like she was looking at me and saying I was someone different from who she thought I was. And I felt pissed off, but that just lasted a day or two. Then I calmed down, and we talked about it again. I thought, *What does it mean for me to abandon this idea?* Well, not a whole lot. Besides, what attracted me to her, even before we got together, is that she's a ballsy broad, and she's smart and opinionated. So if I am going to begrudge her for speaking truthfully because it isn't convenient or because it doesn't suit my view of this particular situation, then that would be a real cop-out.

She suggested that we do something together. And then my best man and one of her bridesmaids said they would take care of it.

Now, had someone said to me—without my fiancée around— three months before our wedding, "Why don't you have a coed bachelor party?" I would have said, "Nah, I don't want to do that." Because it would have felt like the antithesis of what this experience was supposed to be. But like anything in life, it is what you make of it. And what we made from it was a shared experience, and we had a great time and got over that hurdle.

In the end, after male-only and female-only dinners, Gregory, his fiancée, and all of their drunken, altered friends met up at an erotic/comedy cabaret, which included both male and female striptease acts. Ironically, Gregory's head ended up in the cleavage of a busty lady and his wife-to-be was brought on stage to whip a naked cowboy with a belt. "There was a sexual tone to it, but it was all fun and games," notes Gregory. "And clearly nothing was going to get out of hand."

So, how did we get here? To co-ed bashes and five-day bachelor getaways? To side jobs and undercover brides? The next chapter provides some clues and insights about the history of the ritual.

Chapter 2

The More Things Change, the More They Stay the Same

ONLY IN THE LAST COUPLE OF CENTURIES HAS romance become a part of the marriage equation. Once upon a time, people typically didn't get married because they were in love. Marriage was a contract, a coming together of assets, a means of keeping one's genes in the right pool—and in some cases that's still what it's about. Funny thing is, the bond of matrimony might have been stronger and more essential when the institution was lighter on sentiment and emotion. Now there are a variety of paths to attaining and maintaining wealth and status. And, more significant, divorces are readily available and largely acceptable.

Bachelor parties have been around almost as long as people have been getting hitched. The ritual originated in ancient Sparta around 500 B.C., when soldiers would gather before the wedding of one of their own. The groom would entertain his friends with an elaborate feast, during which men toasted one another and the soon-to-be-wed pledged his continued loyalty to his brothers-in-arms.

This basic routine—men eating, drinking, and toasting one another—is remarkably similar to American bachelor dinners of the nineteenth and early twentieth centuries. These dinners frequently appeared in the society pages of local and national newspapers, alongside engagement and birth announcements, with nary a mention of the X-rated bits we've come to associate with the rite. That said, in 1896, Clinton Barnum Seeley's Manhattan stag party was raided by the police, who heard there would be nude female entertainment. In fact, belly dancer Little Egypt remained fully clothed. Still, her appearance at the party, and at a subsequent trial, make the front page of newspapers across the country.

It's hard to know precisely when strippers and the more salty elements became a standard part of the goings-on. "As you can imagine, the history is pretty sketchy," explains Professor Joseph Slade of Ohio University, who is an expert on the history of stag films, those pre-video, black-and-white movies that were once the naughty centerpiece of bachelor parties.

THE ORIGINAL BACHELOR
Henry B.

A trace of stag-party strippers can be found in the archives of the Federal Writers' Project of the Work Progress Administration (also known as the WPA). From 1935 to 1939, during the Great Depression, the WPA paid unemployed writers to interview everyday Americans about their lives. These oral histories offer an intimate and unvarnished look at life in the United States at the beginning of the twentieth century. The WPA interview with Henry B.[1], who was born in Woonsocket, Rhode Island, "in a basement" in 1898, suggests that guys have been having a sex-tinged last hurrah for some time—and that your great-granddad may have partied more than you suspected.

In September 1917, I was drafted for the army. And the night before I left, my friends held a party for me. It was a wild party with everyone drinking, telling stories, and singing. I was sent to Camp Dix, New Jersey, and after a few weeks' training I found myself on board a boat bound for France. I came through [World War I] without a scratch. When I was demobilized, I returned to Woonsocket.

I went to work in the Woonsocket Rubber Co. as a trucker. This job only paid twenty-two dollars [a week], but I was compensated in another way, for while working there I met the girl that later became my wife.

In 1922 the mills started running full-time and I was able to obtain employment as a weaver in the Montrose Mill. Shortly after I started working there, I married Alice. I was twenty-four years old and [she] was twenty

Two nights before the wedding, my friends held a stag party for me. They hired a hall, and about one hundred men gathered

....

1 Library of Congress, Manuscript Division, WPA Federal Writers' Project Collection

there to celebrate my marriage. Father Didion, my pastor, who knew everything that happened in the parish, arrived at the hall early, and, to the consideration of the other guests, he sat down and started eating. After the meal he made a short speech as to the duties of a married man. He then proposed a toast to the young couple and showed that he was the soul of discretion by announcing that it was getting late and he had some duties to attend to at the parish house. Then he left.

Everyone in the hall felt relieved, as most of the acts that they had hired in Boston were of the "strip-tease" type and it was not possible to have them performed while good Father was in the hall.

What Would Emily Do?

In 1922, Emily Post published *Etiquette*[2], commenting on everything from how to answer the door to proper use of the finger bowl. Here's what she had to say about the "bachelor dinner":

A man's dinner is sometimes called a "stag" or a "bachelor" dinner; and as its name implies, is a dinner given by a man and for men only. The best-known bachelor dinner is the one given by the groom just before his wedding. Popularly supposed to have been a frightful orgy, and now arid as the Sahara desert and quite as flat and dreary, the bachelor dinner was in truth

2 Post, Emily. *Etiquette in Society, in Business, in Politics and at Home.* New York: Funk & Wagnalls, 1922.

more often than not a sheep in wolf's clothing.

Aside from toasting the bride, the groom's farewell dinner is exactly like any other "man's dinner," the details depending upon the extravagance or the frugality of the host, and upon whether his particular friends are staid citizens of sober years or mere boys full of the exuberance of youth. Usually there is music of some sort, or "Neapolitans" or "coons" who sing, or two or three instrumental pieces. Often the dinner is short and all go to the theater.

THE POST-WAR BACHELOR
Izzy S.

The history of bachelor parties is also the history of sexuality and gender, and, more specifically, the narrowing of differences between men and women. But history is rarely linear: From the 1920s until World War II, for instance, American women became increasingly independent, attending college and entering the workforce in greater numbers. And with the men off fighting the Nazis, it was up to the women to fill those jobs.

Everything changed when the war ended in 1945: Soldiers returned home to reclaim their positions and commit to their long-lost loves. After years of being apart, these young couples married at an unprecedented rate. While bachelor parties existed prior to 1945, especially among the upper classes, they seemed to gain critical mass in this postwar wedding frenzy.

And that's precisely when Izzy S., an octogenarian snowbird with an accent that's pure Borscht Belt, attended his first stag.

The big deal in 1945, '46, was to have a get-together for the guy that was getting married and a bunch of other guys. And they'd go to a room in a hotel, or a hall in the Masons or the Knights of Pythias. And they invited a couple of broads. And the broads would shed their clothes and did whatever you required of them. People would have sex on the floor. They had all kinds of sexual relations with the women, as far as they wanted to go. And *that* was the big explosion!

There were also times when five of us would get together and hire a car. Somebody was gonna get married, so we said, "Meet us Friday night. We'll get you back for the wedding Saturday afternoon." So Friday night, after work, five guys would get into the car and go to Scranton, Pennsylvania, where there was a red-light district. It was like the red-light district in Holland: The women were outside, and you could see who, what, when, and where.

You'd come back from Scranton about twelve o'clock at night. You'd go to the Russian/Turkish baths. You'd shower or shave, get a massage or a rubdown. You could go swimming. Normally people sat and played cards all night long. And then they had cots where the fellas could sleep.

The big deal back then—it doesn't sound like much at the present time—was dirty pictures. Stag films. You couldn't get 'em. Now you can go on Forty-second Street and rent and see whatever you want. In those days, these things weren't that open; they weren't that available. But those films educated guys. So you would know what a woman looks like and what takes place in marriage. It's hard to conceive how naive people were in those days.

We didn't do anything for my bachelor party. Just a bunch of guys got together and had a couple of drinks. You gotta realize, there was no money around in those days. I worked for eight dollars a week. Twenty cents an hour. It was the time of the war. And I remember people—you might think I'm kidding you—living on the piers. Cooking in a kettle, living in a shack. We at least had an apartment.

Now people fly to Vegas for their friends' bachelor parties. In my times, you stayed home. If you went somewhere, your wife went along. Once you're married, there's no more bachelor. Nowadays, everybody looks for the chance to celebrate, for something to run away to do; it's become important. In my day, it was insignificant. I don't blame these guys. Any doctor, any lawyer, anytime they have a convention, where are they meeting? In Las Vegas! *It's a tax write-off. Let's go to Las Vegas.*

Origin: Lady Jumping Out of Cake

In the seventeenth century, pastry chefs delighted diners with surprise-filled pies that contained flying birds and jumping frogs. That spectacle evolved into the now-legendary lady-jumping-out-of-cake routine, which was repopularized in 1895, when an image of a girl jumping out of a pie at a bachelor dinner hosted by architect Stanford White appeared on the front page of a New York paper—and quickly became the talk of the town. In 1997, an Italian stripper suffocated after waiting inside the *sealed* wooden cake for more than an hour.

Infamous Bachelor Parties:

JIMMY STEWART, 1949

Jimmy Stewart held his bachelor party at legendary Hollywood hangout Chasen's. The highlight of this partly televised affair was two midgets, dressed only in diapers, popping out of a silver serving dish. Now that's class!

CLINTON BARNUM SEELEY, 1896

Captain George Chapman raided the high-society stag of P.T. Barnum's nephew after his precinct received a tip that Little Egypt would be performing naked. Those involved denied anything untoward occurred and cried police misconduct. Chapman was put on trial, and the public was shocked as party details emerged, including the groping of young women, exposing of genitals, and presence of syringes. Chapman was exonerated; Little Egypt became a burlesque legend.

THE UN-BACHELOR
Ernie G.

Definitely with liquor, sometimes with strippers—it's striking how similar the bachelor parties of yore are to today's parties, given how much the world has changed. But many of Izzy's contemporaries, like Ernie G., didn't partake in the ritual, because it was not yet a required stop on the matrimony express.

Ernie got married in 1956. Even though he didn't have an official bachelor party, the night before his wedding suggests how "the last night of freedom" became the raison d'être for the party—which is ironic, since these days couples tend to live together before marriage and men surrender a lot less freedom *at* the altar than Ernie did back in the fifties.

We did everything that we were supposed to do: We went steady, we courted, we kissed, we touched, and that's where it ended. Then we became engaged and went through the engagement process. And the family comes and gives you coffeepots and toasters and blankets and stuff like that. And you save them, and you get married, and you move to an apartment.

We got married in '56. I didn't have a bachelor party. I came from an era where there were no bachelor parties. That was something from the eighties. It was not something in the fifties—at least not where I grew up.

The night before my wedding, I just dropped my wife off at her home—we both lived on the Lower East Side of Manhattan. And I went to this candy store where my friends hung out, and we played cards. We played rummy—five cents, ten cents, and fifteen cents; that was a lot of money in 1956.

They all knew I was gonna get married—half of them were invited to the wedding—but there was no party. It was a regular night; I was just going to the place where all my friends were.

As a matter of fact, here's what happened. Now these memories are coming back to me. I walk in, and these friends of mine are playing cards. And, you know, the guys kid around, saying, "You know, Ernie, you could still back out; you don't have any ropes around your neck, any chains on your feet." Then this friend of mine said to me, "Play my hand. I have to go to the bathroom." So I sat down like thirty seconds before these two guys walked in; I realized right away that they were plainclothed cops.

Before we knew it, there were about eight of us in the paddy wagon [and we were arrested for gambling]. I laugh now, but I really didn't know if I was gonna be out before my wedding. And I told the detective who locked us up that I was getting married the next day. Did he care? He said, "Oh, you may have to stay here till Monday. The judge is off." I was such a nervous wreck. I thought I was gonna be in jail for my wedding night.

But he was torturing me. We went to night court and they brought us up before the judge. Somebody from the neighborhood brought a lawyer to get us out.

I was twenty-two, twenty-three years old when I got married. And then your life changes: You go from total freedom to a life of . . . you know, you start another life with somebody else. It's not easy. I mean, I never went back to the candy store to play cards. Nope. Never. Because I . . . I . . . I had my wife. I had responsibilities. We had this family restaurant, and that took care of a lot of my time. I put in sixteen hours a day. And when I closed up at night, when I went home, I fell asleep. That was my day.

THE FIFTIES BACHELOR
Joe V.

As Brett Harvey points out in *The Fifties: A Women's Oral History*[3], men and women were getting married earlier and in greater numbers in the 1950s—and for good reason. "For the majority of American women, their sexual initiation took place within the framework of marriage," she explains. "In fact, marriage was often the only way for a woman to have sex." Keep in mind, birth-control pills were not introduced into the United States until 1960, and safe abortions were hard to come by. In other words, there was nothing casual about sex. Of course, some men and women were having sex before marriage, but in the 1950s, if word got out, the women were branded "bad girls" and were less desirable as wives. That double standard certainly informed Italian-American Joe V.'s thinking as he chose a bride in 1959.

There was no sex before we got married. I had done it, but not with her. Usually when I dated a girl, if I didn't really particularly want to marry her, I would put a move on her. But if I wanted to marry her, I wanted that honeymoon to be exactly what it should be, or at least what I thought it should be.

I met my wife through her brother. He was a buddy of mine. And when I met her, I knew that she was probably gonna be the one. I just knew. And, of course, this is before I went into

---

3 Harvey, Brett. *The Fifties: A Women's Oral History.* New York: HarperCollins, 1993.

the service[4]. So I wrote to her occasionally, and when I came back . . . that was it.

I had been to a few stags before mine. Like most of the stags I'd been to, I thought that they would have a stripper at mine. My best man was a very, very close friend of mine. He set up the stag. He did a pretty good job, we had a lot of people come. It was at a hotel in New Haven. And there was a dinner. And then there were strippers. And that was it.

Most of the stags I've been to, people didn't get that crazy, because they had to pay for their own drinks. It's different from going to a wedding where somebody's paying for the booze. Usually you go, you have a drink; at my stag I bought a few of my friends a drink, but that was basically it.

I do remember the stripper. She was not very young. In 1959, the type of female who stripped was completely different from the strippers that they have lately. Back then it was an older woman. She was not as nice. It was not like she was a Playboy Bunny. The one that I had was old; I was very disappointed. She looked like shit! [*laughs*] My best man got her; evidently he didn't spend too much money.

What happened? They announced her, my best man put on a record, and bingo, she just went around and maybe teased some people. Then it was over; she left. That particular time, she didn't go into another room and, uh, service[5] anybody.

I think stags have changed from that standpoint. As years went on, they got a little crazier. You could have a raffle: In some

4 **service** (n) the armed forces of a nation
5 **service** (v) performance of a nonspecific sexual act, sometimes for money

cases people bought a ticket, and if you won, you would go into the backroom with the stripper.

I went to one, it's gotta be at least twenty-five years ago. There was a bunch of Italians at this particular stag. It was in one of these halls, a typical Italian hall. There must have been one hundred and fifty people. The guy who got married sold the veal in the neighborhood and they had an Italian restaurant—so the food was dynamite.

When the dinner was over, in came the entertainment. My dad's nephew—my cousin—was the one getting married. And actually, my dad was sitting in the front row. He's gotta be in at least his late sixties, maybe early seventies, at that point. And they had two or three girls who came out. This one girl in particular, redhead, started sitting on my dad's lap, and did the teasing bit. And my dad started getting all excited, as well as the groom.

So it comes to the end of the show, and the girl starts taking her clothes off, and she takes her top off. And I'm looking: redhead, nice body, very attractive, but something wasn't right. I mean, I picked up on it. She takes off the bottom, and she's got a *shvantz*[6] this long!

Wow! The whole place went crazy! These Italians went out of their minds. They felt like they were taken advantage of. They were deceived, okay? It was pandemonium! Some of these guys were jumping off their chairs and screaming. They had to get "her"—or "it" or "him"—out of there really quick. The best man, who set the thing up, just laughed.

Nobody has ever forgotten that stag. I just had my buddy over who was at that particular stag party and we were talking about it; he remembered the food *and* that stripper.

I was actually best man for a person who got married in maybe '68 or '69. And I didn't have a stripper. I had like a roast. And I presented the groom with a plaque. "So-and-so hereby relinquishes his bachelorhood. Dated such and such, witnessed by the best man and all the groomsmen in the wedding." And I had other people come up and talk. That was a little different. I wanted him to make as much money as he could. I didn't spend money on strippers and stuff, so whatever I collected, we gave to the groom.

Origin: Groomsmen

Dressed in matching tuxes and standing beside the groom, groomsmen have become visual accessories to the modern wedding ceremony—about as important as an appendix (and just as likely to erupt). But that hasn't always been the case. Back in the Dark Ages[7], if there were no wedding prospects in one's tribe, a man and his friends and family might invade a neighboring community and capture a bride. It was up to the groom's kin to fend off any challenges from the bride's family and clear a path for the couple's escape.

....

7 **Dark Ages** aka the European Early Middle Ages (from about A.D. 476 to about 1000); sometimes used pejoratively to suggest the Middle Ages lacked significant cultural achievements

In many cultures, men and women in the wedding party still dress identically to the bride and groom to confuse the evil spirits, who may seek to harm the newlyweds—or so the superstition goes.

You see, to go to the stag party, usually you had to have a ticket. You paid for it, because somebody had to pay for the dinner, and you had to guarantee a certain amount of dinners. The ticket could be anywhere from fifteen dollars to about thirty dollars. And if they had gambling, they took a piece of the pot and saved it for the groom. Then sometimes they raffled things off—liquor, things of that nature. It was all to make money for the groom, so that he gets some cash, because he was going to spend money for his wedding and to buy things for his apartment. It's the same thing for the bridal shower. They do it so that the female will get some gifts.

I actually went to a dance once in New Haven in the fifties and there was a group of women. One of the girls was about to get married and she was out for her last single night—sowing her oats, so to speak. I didn't think too much of it at the time, but that wasn't done back then; those girls were way ahead of their time.

Origin: The Bachelorette Party

A byproduct of the sexual revolution of the late 1960s and the women's liberation movement of the 1970s, the bachelorette party began as an eye-for-an-eye response to the bachelor party.

Before then, brides were presumed virgins, so there was no reason to mark her last night of sexual freedom.

According to Dr. Beth Montemurro, author of *Something Old, Something Bold*, "While there is evidence that the bachelorette party has been around since the 1960s, there is nothing to suggest that it was formally labeled as such or identified as a ritual and expected part of the engagement period until the mid-1980s or early 1990s."[8] No doubt, the penis straw and condom veil were born soon thereafter.

THE ODD COUPLE
Jon B. & Ted W.

In 1953, Hugh Heffner began publishing *Playboy* (which was going to be called *Stag Party* until an existing outdoor magazine named *Stag* threatened to sue). And in 1960, he opened the first Playboy Club in Chicago. As late as 1957 the U.S. Supreme Court was still sending purveyors of porn to prison, and books like D. H. Lawrence's *Lady Chatterley's Lover* and Henry Miller's *Tropic of Cancer* were routinely banned and deemed obscene by the courts and law enforcement. But in less than a decade, the U.S. Supreme Court and those of individual states would overturn the most conservative obscenity laws, declaring that creation and distribution of sexual materials was protected by the First Amendment so long as they

8 Montemurro, Beth. *Something Old, Something Bold: Bridal Showers and Bachelor Parties.* New Jersey: Rutgers University Press, 2006.

had "the slightest redeeming social importance."

The point: Sexual mores were in a state of flux in the United States at this time. And, after more than a decade of clear moral guidelines, mixed messages were being sent to young adults. That may explain why Jon B.'s and Ted W.'s recollections of Ted's bachelor party in 1964—and the prevailing notions of sex at the time—differ, sometimes dramatically.

Ted: When Jon and I were at Michigan State University, the girls' dorms were locked down during the week at ten p.m., and at eleven thirty on the weekends—and they had bed checks. In the building that we lived in, one Sunday a month they had the boys' dorms open and the girls could come in. Of course, all the doors were open and the R.A. would walk up and down the halls, and everyone's feet had to be on the floor. We were coming from that. And all of a sudden you have a stag party with cigar smoke and dancing and naked girls and card playing; it was like Alice fell through the hole into Wonderland.

I really didn't know what to expect before the party; I just knew that there'd be girls. I knew that there'd be a crowd of probably one hundred and twenty-five people. All I had to do was invite my friends; everything else was being taken care of.

It was at a synagogue. My father-in-law and a couple of his brothers arranged it; one uncle was a bartender and he knew who to contact for the dancers and stuff like that. And my father-in-law's business was in Detroit, so he knew that he'd be able to get protection and we weren't gonna be raided because of whatever was going to be happening. You don't hear about stags being raided nowadays, but back then it was big-time.

Infamous Bachelor Parties:
KENNETH REEVES, 1969

Judge **Edward Haggerty** presided over the **John F. Kennedy** assassination trial of **Clay L. Shaw**, who was acquitted. A few years later, the judge was the one in legal trouble after a bachelor party he helped organize for Kenneth Reeves was busted. Haggerty was arrested for "organizing an assemblage for indecent purposes, procuring lewd films and photographs, and procuring prostitutes." While he was found not guilty on the basis that the party was a private function, he was removed from the bench a year later.

Jon: Ted was a good friend. He was dating this girl from high school on, and he finally decided to get married, and he asked me to be his best man. His father-in-law was a fairly crazy guy, and he had two brothers that were much crazier than he was. And they were planning the stag. It was ironic, because usually you don't have the bride's side set something up like that.

The uncles probably thought, *We're gonna make sure our new nephew gets his rocks off, his last hurrah.* They were also probably showing off. I remember watching these uncles at the party; they had these weird smirks on their faces. I had never seen adults acting like that. It was both humorous and pathetic. Why make a big deal out of this? But they did pull it off. You know, they did get the whores.

Ted: Most bachelor parties at that time were somewhat of a profit-making thing. It was like twenty-five or thirty dollars to get in; and you had the food and the booze. After the expenses, whatever was left went to the bachelor. So the more people that came, the more the bachelor made. I must have gotten, shit, like five hundred dollars. That was like two, three weeks pay—and that was the whole point.

But I had no idea what the hell was going on. I was twenty-one and overwhelmed with the number of people there, the level of noise, the number of card games being played, people just shoveling down booze.

And when the curtains on the stage opened, our eyes were bulging out; we were in disbelief. There were a couple of mattresses on the stage and these three women just in high heels.

I think there were two black girls and a white girl. It's hard to believe: It's been like forty years, but I remember one was kind of heavy. And none of them were pretty.

Jon: They weren't fabulous looking. They weren't fat or anything; they had reasonably decent bodies. But it was like, you know, "What is this all about? What am I doing here?"

Ted: The girls did some half-assed dance routine, just a poor quality, low-end-hooker strip routine. I know the girls got fifty bucks each, which I guess was a lot of money—plus what they made on the side. They were charging for blow jobs or whatever onstage and behind the curtain.

After the introductions, I basically hung out with my friends, because then the party was on automatic pilot: Everybody was pursuing whatever their pleasures were, whether it was cards or drinking or bullshitting around or the girls.

And there was a lot of business being done. Actually, there were some big Fortune 500 guys there. I remember somebody had just consummated a big business deal and one of them was walking across the stage—and I don't even know how he got up there—but the girls started undressing him. Then a couple of the guys yelled, "Jesus Christ, get him off the stage." Because the whole business deal could have gone into the toilet if he ended up in a compromising situation.

Some of the older guys, they might have been in their fifties, went up there or behind the curtains. The younger guys, our age or a little bit older, just got into the dance routines with the girls. I wouldn't have felt comfortable going up onstage, no matter how drunk I was or how much I would have maybe wanted to. My wife's uncles did try to make me go onstage at the beginning, but they finally realized that it wasn't going to happen—and I think my father went over to them and told them to, you know, back off.

All of my friends were hesitant too. We hung around together for dear life—not knowing how far to venture out away from own little sphere of influence. So we were bonding big-time among ourselves. Like, you know, "What should we do? How inappropriate can we be or not be? And what's going to happen to us?" Besides embarrassment, there's the possibility of disease or something like that. You had things like syphilis and the clap[9]; we didn't know what we were talking about, but we were afraid and trying to justify or rationalize

9 the clap (n) *slang*, gonorrhea

it. I mean, we were pretty conservative. Ozzie and Harriet—that was
the world that was going on.

All of a sudden you have a stag party with cigar smoke and dancing and naked girls and card playing; it was like Alice fell through the hole into Wonderland.

Jon: We had all gone to whorehouses. For five bucks, we figured,
that's cheaper than a date. We'd go find these prostitutes that we
heard about and go to these gang bangs. We had fraternity parties in
high school where we brought in two prostitutes. I remember once
this guy's parents were out of town and the grandmother was up in
her bedroom and we did it at his house. You'd walk down the stairs,
and for five bucks you could get a half-and-half—that's a blow job
and a fuck. It was fabulous!

But Ted's party was something that these older guys had set
up, bringing the prostitutes to us—that was the part of the stag that
was absolutely derelict.

If I remember, Ted didn't get up onstage; he was more or less getting all these other clowns to. He somehow got a hold of my car keys and threw them up onto the stage. And he said, "Okay, Jon, go get your keys." And these women were like piranhas. And I was freaking out. I was totally wiped-out drunk, also. So I had to crawl up on that stage, finally grabbing my keys. And they were grabbing at me. I made it off the stage and I was cussing everybody out. I was sort of scared and embarrassed. At the same time, I was totally out of it. I remember going home and my friends helped me up the steps to my bedroom, and I threw up all over my room. My mom was not really happy with me.

Ted: I must've left at maybe one o'clock in the morning, and things were still going on. There was still a group waiting in line to hook up with the girls, and guys playing cards. I ended up driving home with my older brother and my father. When I got home, I wondered what happened to Jon. It seemed relevant and important to me at the time.

Jon: I didn't do anything with the girls. I didn't want to pay the money—and I thought it was going to be a public spectacle. And I was probably shy. I'd gone to prostitutes before, so that was no big deal, but usually there's a little privacy. Plus I probably had so much booze in me I may not have been able to get it up.

Ted: It was almost like a fantasy world, because dancers weren't something that were readily available in the Detroit market at that point. Still, I think my wife pretty much knew what was going to happen. But here's a twenty-year-old girl who was graduating as a teacher. And we were getting married. I think what was in her mind and what happened in reality were two completely different things. She thinks, *Well, there's going to be dancers there.* But how does that translate?

I don't think she thought there would be prostitutes. I mean, it's hard to put yourself in that time frame and remember the innocence of things; most girls got married and moved from their parents' home into their own home. There was really no such thing as a transition. That's just what you did.

BOYS ON FILM: PART I

From the very beginning of cinema, filmmakers have been inspired by bachelors and their last hurrah. Here's a sampling of movies from the pre-Hanks era:

His Bachelor Dinner (1915)

Captain Kidd's Kids (1919)

The Ace of Cads (1926)

The Body Disappears (1941)

The Bachelor Party (1957; nominated for an Academy Award)

How to Murder Your Wife (1965)

The Ecstasies of Women (1969)

THE EXPERT
Professor Joseph Slade

The adventures of Ted and Jon, Joe, Ernie, and Izzy track quite closely to Professor Joseph Slade's understanding of the evolution of the bachelor party. And he suggests that, as much as the ritual has changed over the years, a more drastic revolution may be afoot.

By the sixties, bachelor parties became considerably more graphic; it became much more commonplace to bring in prostitutes, for example. There is a lot more pressure on the groom to have intercourse with one of them. Prior to that time, while it doubtless happened, I don't think it was quite as institutionalized. But I think, because of the sixties and because of the growing liberalization and the so-called sexual revolution, actual sex became a lot more common at these parties.

And the ritual became more public, in the sense that everybody knew about it by then. And it became more self-conscious. Prior to that, it was still beneath the social radar. Because once that happens, once the culture acknowledges it, then I suspect expectations are being raised, such as [the number or quality of] the strippers or prostitutes or more drunkenness. It's just license to up the ante a little bit. And my sense is that the parties have become more expensive and more status-conscious, and that you have better liquors and that sort of thing.

I think coed bachelor parties are just a natural progression. There seems to be a growing consensus that, in general, gender doesn't matter quite as much. And as females have made inroads into professional life and business, there has really been less and less justification to keep them out of previously exclusively male clubs. So I think it's logical that men and women would get together for bachelor parties. Whether the parties are still going to be as raucous or not is something else entirely. I've spoken to women who have been to what in effect were bachelor parties and they viewed some of the drunkenness and strippers with considerable distaste.

Of course, that's not the case with all women. Still, the incorporation of female friends and joined bachelor/bachelorette parties changes the ritual. For one thing, female friends may serve as a natural ally for grooms who'd prefer to skip the strip clubs. And most bachelors will probably be on better—if not their best—behavior if females are around. Only time will tell. In the meantime, let's take a closer look at the ritual's more recent and sordid past, starting with the main attraction—and I don't mean the groom.

Chapter 3

That's Entertainment!

THEY'VE SEEN HUNDREDS AND IN SOME CASES THOU-sands of men celebrate the ritual. They've seen it all or, more to the point, the same thing—over and over and over. They're the strippers and drivers, dwarves and naughty clowns, paint-ball park owners, and other purveyors of good times that make their livelihoods at the moral and financial center of the modern bachelor party.

Whether it's a day of shooting paint-filled bullets or a night of erotic shenanigans, most bachelor parties (and bachelor-ette parties, for that matter) are planned bonding experiences that leave little wiggle room for spontaneity. Even seemingly outrageous acts are somewhat predictable. (Cue the married father of two paying an underage prostitute twenty-five bucks for a blow job in the bathroom.)

Still, the men and women who entertain these unruly masses

have a front-row seat, and some illuminating perspectives, on bachelor parties and the institution that spawned them: marriage. They also have some interesting backstories of their own.

THE TATTOO ARTIST
Wes B.

Wes B. manages a tattoo parlor in New Orleans's French Quarter. While business is finally picking up after Hurricane Katrina decimated the once and future bachelor party destination, Wes still had time to chat about one particularly raucous bachelor party that invaded his tattoo parlor a few years back.

The shop got a call from somebody asking if we could accommodate a large group. We never like doing that; we just prefer to do one or two tattoos at a time, because groups are a pain in the neck. When we found out it was a bachelor party, we said, "Absolutely not!"

But they were determined, and they were like, "We'll just come in anyway." I said, "Well, this is a tattoo shop. You know, we are bad people—you don't want to mess with us. So let's work something out."

We told them it was a now-or-never situation, and they said, "All right then, we will make it worth your while." So they just picked up what they had going on and brought it over; they ended up renting out the shop for the night. We locked the door and they brought their people and these portable stripper poles with lights and, of course, strippers. They also brought a full bar and a couple of tanks of nitrous[1]. It was pretty funny, because nitrous didn't really mix well with the dancers. Strippers aren't usually the most graceful dancers in the world anyway, and the laughing gas was not helping the situation.

It got pretty boisterous. They were drinking drinks off of the girls. I guess if you pour stuff slowly enough it kind of goes in rivulets down, and that seemed to entertain them a lot. Same thing with the balloons of nitrous and the joints they were smoking— they seemed to really enjoy getting as many mouths as possible involved in all those processes.

They all ended up getting these matching tattoos, which were a combination of the bachelor's zodiac sign and the date of the wedding.

There must have been sixteen or seventeen guys. A good half of them were not the type of people who would ever get tattoos or would ever be in tattoo shops. There were a couple that tried to bounce on the thing—there's always one person who is apprehensive, and what I normally do is have him go first. But everybody got them, although I am guessing quite a few of them might not've recalled the tattoos until the next day.

I think it was a bonding thing: The tattoos create some sort of connection between them.

....

1 nitrous *aka laughing gas, nitrous oxide, N_2O, whippits* (n) gas that, when inhaled, causes a temporary light-headedness and sense of ease; typically used by dentists as an anesthetic, and by young adults as a recreational drug

So, have you been to many bachelor parties?

Yeah, I've been to a few. I had a girlfriend who was a dancer, and I would go with her to bachelor parties to make sure the guys didn't try to fuck her. You don't want to think people are stupid and selfish, but they turn out to mostly be that way.

Normally we didn't hang out. Though one time, a group encouraged us to stay. We had a couple of drinks, and I felt a little weird, so I sat down. I was kind of nodding out from whatever was in there, because the guys tried to drug me. My girlfriend woke me up and I woke up swinging, which normally wasn't like me, but it must have been from the drugs, you know, Klonopin or roofies or something. We made it out to the car and got the fuck out of there.

These days, I wouldn't stand for that kind of crap; I just don't want to see my girlfriend with another guy. Whereas when I was younger it didn't really matter to me; I trusted her and I didn't care. But in the long run, I've never met a mentally healthy dancer.

THE LESBIAN STRIPPER
Mary G.

Mary G., is a smart, together stripper turned corporate lawyer. From 1989 to 1991, she danced at bachelor parties in the middle-class and wealthy suburbs of Southern California. While she has seen plenty of esteem-challenged women dance for the compliments and attention of men, she was never one of them. "I was out as a dyke at that point, so I didn't need validation from the

men I was dancing for. For me it was a simple equation: Is it safe? Can I get money?"

There was some fear of the unknown in the beginning, like, "Can I really pull this off? Can I pass as a straight stripper?" It was also performance anxiety: "Is the music going to work? Can I gracefully unclip my bra?" In retrospect, if that's your biggest worry, great.

I was never really worried about my safety, because the psychological dynamics of bachelor parties are similar to almost any group: For every bad person, there's the person who wants to do good; for every person who wants to scare you, there's the person who wants to save you. And if you can identify them, you can usually play them off each other.

The best man, for instance, was usually the point person and the ambassador, and he was the one I would tell, "I am going to end up leaving if you can't keep your friends in line, and I am going to really lean on you. And you have more responsibility, because I trust you. But if your friends cross the line, I'm outta here." And that can be a real downer: Nobody wants to have the stripper running out of the party with half her clothes on; that is not the story you want to tell the next day. Now, as a lawyer, I do these same things to judges that I did to the best man: make them feel like they want to do the right thing and that they are important and special.

At a bachelor party you win or lose people's confidence within the first five minutes. So, to start off, I would walk in and basically outline to everyone, "This is what's going to happen: I'm going to do two sets; the first set is for the bachelor. Then I'm going to take a five-minute break, and then we're going to play tipping games. We'll talk more about that when I come back out."

STRIPPER V. BACHELOR

It's not all fun and games. In fact bachelor parties have been the subject of criminal investigations, alleged murders, assorted crimes, and many lawsuits. Here are the details of two, one suit headed to *The People's Court,* the other settled out of court.

Shimkonis v. Diamond Dolls: In 1998 Paul Shimkonis filed a lawsuit against the Florida strip joint where his bachelor party was held. He claimed that a dancer caused assorted injuries when she thrust her very large breasts into his face, causing his head to jerk backward. He sought $15,000 in damages. But instead of letting a local jury hear his case, Shimkonis opted to have his grievance settled on TV's *The People's Court*, Judge Ed Koch presiding! **THE VERDICT:** Diamond Dolls, Not Guilty.

Scheidt v. Showgirl III: In 2003 Justin Scheidt sued an Indiana strip club, claiming he was seriously injured after being brought up onstage—per his "friends'" request—during his bachelor party. He alleged two dancers held him down while a third cannonballed six feet down a strip pole, landing "squarely on his genitals, causing him excruciating pain." He claimed that he begged the trio to stop, but they refused; instead they took turns jumping on him. The bachelor, who was married just hours later, contended that the injuries he sustained made it impossible to perform his matrimonial duties on the honeymoon.

THE VERDICT: After turning down a $10,000 offer, Scheidt settled out of court in 2005 for an undisclosed sum.

When I tell people I used to work at bachelor parties, they say, "Oh my gosh, that must have been so chaotic, being in a room full of one hundred men." It actually was very structured and more than half the time these guys were scared shitless—so much more nervous than I could ever be—and actually not really even sexualizing the whole experience; it would end up being more of an anatomy class. And they were nervous about being around explicit sexuality with their peers looking at them. They were worried about how they were responding: Are they into it appropriately or are they not into it appropriately? Each and every person in the room was so self-conscious.

I was actually surprised that so many men know so little about female anatomy. I would do vibrator shows and the guys would go and get flashlights. It became not so much an erotic thing; it was more like, "What? That's a vagina?" And these are guys that are about to get married! These are doctors, attorneys, cops, firefighters, feds, frat boys, professors, military people, engineers, bikers, farm workers—anyone and everyone you could imagine.

When we got into the tipping games, the erotic thrill was a little bit more between them. It was, "I'm going to give you five dollars to go and do that to my friend." It wasn't so much "me, me, me"; it was more, "I want to see my friend either squirm or have to do something sexual."

For one dollar, I would take that dollar from anywhere. Typically people would tuck it into the top of their pants or their button-down shirt, or put it in their mouth. There was a lot of unsanitary money exchanging going on. For five dollars they could lick whipped cream off of a nipple. For ten dollars, they could lick it off both breasts.

Twenty dollars was the clincher; it was called "feed the kitty." I would take the twenty, roll it up like you were going to snort a line, and they would put it in their mouth. I would have them lay on the floor, and I would crouch over them and I would pick it up with my vagina; there was absolutely no contact, just with the money. I practiced it beforehand with my girlfriend. It didn't take very long to perfect it, but I did figure out exactly how it needed to be rolled up and exactly how much of the twenty needed to be in his mouth in order to do the trick without any contact. And then, by literally looking up at my own vagina with a mirror, I figured out how to do it in a somewhat erotic way. That was the big money-maker—always.

I probably did about a hundred fifty bachelor parties in three years. But every party was the same. You had the same stuff, the same attitude; the guys were interchangeable.

And then I was out of there—hopefully one thousand dollars wealthier. No, that's not true; sometimes there were other offers that got worked out beforehand or when I announced the tipping games.

Basically, you're chasing the money; you negotiate the fee, and part of it is gauging—how much do these people have? If you over-shoot, you lose the whole deal. You know, sixty bucks, one hundred bucks, one hundred fifty bucks, whatever it was—and I would set a certain time limit, one song. If they want another song, "Okay, another eighty bucks."

> Sometimes I would pretend to orgasm. If men actually knew how women orgasm, they would have been like, "That is so fake."

There could be an oil-and-vibrator show. Usually the vibrator show was, let me put oil on myself and then I will lay on the ground and writhe to the music and turn a vibrator on, lick it, and put it in my vagina. Again, they'd get out the flashlights and were fascinated with, "How big is the vibrator? Is it bigger than my dick? How much can fit in a vagina?"

Sometimes I would pretend to orgasm. And when we did two-woman shows—they never called it a lesbian show—I would always have an "orgasm" with the friend that I worked with; we would almost be laughing. We would grind on each other and we would time it like, "Okay, now." If men actually knew how women orgasm, they would have been like, "That is so fake."

I probably did about a hundred fifty bachelor parties in three years. Sometimes there would be three on Friday night and three on Saturday night. Other weekends, nothing—it was very seasonal. But every party was the same: You had the same stuff, the same attitude; the guys were interchangeable.

But every party was also a little outrageous, because you got this little glance into these people's lives and their environment. For example, I did a show for these farm workers in the middle of this field on their machinery. That was my stage—this flatbed truck and the machinery. The most uncomfortable one was for these professors from the university where I was a student. Superuncomfortable—too close to home. And one time we did a show at a phenomenal winery. It was a superextravagant party, because these people owned the winery and had a mansion on the property. They laid down probably three to four grand for two of us, and gave us each a case of wine.

But whether it was at a winery or on a flatbed truck, it was the same thing, the same dynamic. And it really was a great job: I was independent, there was no time commitment, I made great money. I was in and out in an hour and never saw the people again. In my non-sex-work life, it's like going to a conference, doing a presentation and leaving, versus going to work every day in the same place. It allowed me the flexibility to do the other things—like get through law school.

Once Mary got her law degree, she stopped dancing. "My only regret is that I didn't save more money," she admits.

"Instead me and my girlfriend ate sushi every night. It was good living, really good living."

THE GUILTY STRIPPER
June T.

June T. felt rejected and dejected after her divorce. "My ex-husband left me for a woman who could be more doting and give him more attention and sex and all those sensual things," explains the ex-cheerleader and practicing personal trainer. She started stripping to support her daughter after her marriage ended. Because she doesn't want other women to go through the same painful experience, she teaches the tricks of her trade to the ladies in her small New England town. (Plus she feels a little guilty about dancing for their men.)

I do feel a gentle sort of moral responsibility or karmic responsibility to the wives, fiancées, and girlfriends. I feel like I'm stealing something they should be having. He shouldn't be giving me compliments about whatever part of my body; he should be giving his partner those compliments. If he gave his wife forty bucks so she could go out and have two hours to herself for a manicure and pedicure, I swear to God that she would come home and give him an awesome hummer.[2] Instead he is giving forty bucks to me to shake it over him and touch my own breasts. In many cases, his

....

2 **hummer** (n) *slang*, blow job

wife is too tired to have sex, because she made dinner, did laundry, and maybe even mowed the lawn. That's one of the reasons I teach something called The Strippers Workout. It helps women reestablish and regain a sense of sensuality and sexuality.

Men go to strip clubs to see some girl that put her game on, who put on some fucking panties and some high-heeled shoes. One of the biggest misconceptions is that strippers are all exotic beauties; I have been in rooms with some wide-assed girls with cellulite thighs. But they are comfortable with themselves. They will touch themselves, be free with themselves. And a lot of women are not.

I see some women who are driving around in their sweatpants, dragging their kids. I mean, take five minutes—put some lip gloss on and brush your hair. Get rid of your fanny ass and pussy gut.[3] You're not doing anything to make yourself feel on top of your game.

THE ENTREPRENEUR
Danny X.

Danny X. knows how lucrative bachelor party entertainment can be. He's an entrepreneur who, as he sees it, just happens to make his living booking dancers for bachelor and bachelorette parties, as well as birthdays and anniversaries. It all began when a friend suggested there was money to be made. "But I didn't consider it a real business, and, you know, I told him he

---

3 **pussy gut** (n) *slang*, belly some women retain after giving birth

was crazy." Eleven years and thousands of parties later, Danny has built Centerfold Strips, a national company that employs talent—including dwarves, male dancers, and "fat mamas"— in most major American cities. He recalls his early days in the business: It all started when he posted a help-wanted ad for dancers at his gym. "Sure enough, a week later a girl called me. I met with her and she became my first employee."

Before I knew it, I had several dancers working for me. So I printed up some business cards on my computer and started passing them out in the parking lots of nightclubs and shopping centers, and clients started calling me to book these dancers. My first year in this business, there was a big learning curve, because I was never in the adult industry; I was coming from the parking-garage business. So I was out every weekend attending the bachelor parties, making sure the clients were happy and the entertainers were happy. I learned a lot about the dynamics of a party and what the guys are looking for. And of course a lot of times the guys are looking for something extra, above and beyond dancing—and our company does *not* provide that service.

There is really a thin line between dancing and escorting. And a lot of the dancers cross over the line, and a lot of the escorts promote that they do bachelor parties, where, you know, they don't entertain, but they "take care of business." So sometimes that line gets a little blurred.

I guess I didn't clarify it enough at first, so I would have twenty-five guys at a bachelor party coming over to me saying, "Can we get extras from the girls?" "How much is this?" and "How much is that?" I would sort of be like, "I'm sorry guys, we don't do that." And they're like, "The last time we called a company, the girls did it."

I learned quickly to be very forthright when the client calls to book the entertainment. You have to tell them, "This is not an escort service, and we want to let you know in advance that the girls we employ do not do anything 'extra.' If that is the type of service you are looking for, we recommend you call someone else, because we don't want you to be unhappy with the service we're going to provide."

Initially I worked at the parties as a driver.[4] The role of the driver, first and foremost, is to make sure the party is secure and that the girls are safe. I'm also there to help the girls carry their exotic-dancer bag, which would have their clothing, whipped cream, and party accessories, as well as to collect the money from the clients when we get there and to make change for the guys; you know, recirculate the singles.

As the owner, I also made sure the girls didn't hand out any phone numbers to clients or try to take away business from the company. And if the guys wanted to upgrade to a certain type of show, or longer length of time, I would be the one to okay it with the girls.

When I started, I was probably a bit timid and just hung out in the corner and let the girls do their thing. But the girls really do control the flow of the show. They determine how wild or how mild the guys are going to be. Still, as the driver, you want to approach the guys and establish a rapport from the beginning—let them know that you're their friend and you're there to help them. If they think you are their enemy—well, that is not the end of the

---

4 driver (n) also known as a bodyguard or dancer's escort

stick you want to be on. Because if they feel you're a threat to their party and their fun, someone might test you—especially when there's alcohol involved.

I talked to one female dancer who preferred to bring another woman as her driver, as opposed to a man . . .

I prefer drivers to be male, because a male would be more under-standing of another male in that type of position. And if there is a fully clothed female with the girl that's dancing, especially if the guys are intoxicated, they might give her a hard time and say, "Hey, honey, why don't you go out there and dance for us? Let's see what you got." Of course, I would rather have a female driver there than no one.

I think the whole Duke lacrosse scandal could have been avoided if the dancers had a driver with them. He could have got-ten them out of there safely and averted this situation—if it did in fact occur. But it scares me, because if it did happen that means there are people out there that would take it that far. And it puts fear into everyone in the industry: The girls don't feel comfortable with stuff like that in the media, so it's going to be more difficult for me to recruit dancers and retain them. And it makes the guys a little bit on edge, like, "If we have this girl here, who is to say that she won't lie and claim that this happened and that happened?"

What about bachelorette parties? Have you been to any?

What is interesting is that girls can be more rowdy and more aggressive than the guys. This one time, I had a couple of male dancers booked for a bachelorette party at a hotel in the Hamptons[5]. One of the male dancers called me up a few hours prior to the show and said he couldn't do it because he was using some kind of hot-wax hair-removal stuff on his chest and got burned. So I called up the other male dancer and said, "You're on your own tonight; the other guy can't make it." He said, "Why don't you come with me?" And I said, "What am I going to do? I've never been a dancer before." He said, "Just follow my lead."

So I picked him up and we drove out there. When we pulled into the parking lot, there were thirty women on the balcony, and I'm thinking, *Oh my God, I am dead.* So we come walking through the parking lot, and the girls are yelling from the balcony, "Hey, are you guys strippers?" So we say, "No, but if you want us to be, we will be." Just joking around with them. So we come up to the room and maybe five of the girls leave; they didn't want to partake for whatever reason. The remaining twenty-five closed the door and locked it behind us. Before I knew it, I had women clawing at me, ripping my clothes off, pouring whipped cream on my body and eating it off, pouring shots of liquor down my throat—if I didn't experience it, I would be hesitant to believe it.

I think women need more of a fantasy or a story, like, "We're cops and we're here to arrest you." It has to be more of a show than just the guy coming in and stripping. Guys, on the other hand, are really not that picky. They're looking for a hot girl to get naked and give them a lap dance. Although, more and more, guys are asking for the novelty entertainers, such as the midgets and the fat mamas.

....

5 the **Hamptons** (n) a wealthy enclave on the southern tip of Long Island

I am kind of surprised by it. If it was my bachelor party, I would want some hot girls to entertain me, because it's going to be my last night of fun and I am going to be with my wife the rest of my life; I wouldn't want a three-hundred-fifty-pound woman or a midget.

I guess most people have already seen regular hot strippers, whether it's at another bachelor party or a club, so maybe they're looking to do something different. The other thing is, sometimes you need to have a little bit less sexual overtone. And that could be for several reasons, such as pressure from the bride-to-be or the bride's family, or it could be that the guys are really looking to give the bachelor a hard time or joke around with him a little bit.

For many stags, it's not an either/or proposition. Sometimes the "novelty" act is either the opening act or the punch line. One friend told me about a party he planned that included three strippers. The first two were of the *Playboy* variety and the bachelor was loving it. They blindfolded him before they brought out the grand finale. And when they took the blindfold off, well, he vomited all over the morbidly obese stripper.

THE LITTLE PERSON
Scott S.

Being the punch line seems like a hard way to earn a living. So why would someone put themselves in that position? Danny introduced me to one of his company's most popular little people: forty-seven-year-old Scott S., who is four-foot-one-inch tall.

Scott shed some light on the situation and his own motivations. For starters, performing at parties is just his weekend job. Scott also works in a nursing home as a physical therapist. Born and raised in Brooklyn, he now lives in Connecticut with his five-foot-two-inch wife and their eight-year-old daughter. "I make a nice salary at the nursing home," he explains. "I call that my bread and butter. But the parties are my gravy."

I have been in the entertaining business for over twenty years. My big break was in 1985, when I did the *Christmas Spectacular* at Radio City Music Hall: I played the baby bear in the Nutcracker scene, a snowman in the Christmas in New York scene, and I was an elf in the Santa's Workshop scene. I met tons of celebrities through that and networked, and it led to doing soap operas and music videos. I was also in a band called Mini Kiss.

That's how Danny found out about me; he saw me on the band's website and e-mailed me. He said they were looking for a little person to do bachelor and bachelorette parties. My first reaction was "How much?"

I talked it over with some people. And my family questioned me, like, "Are you sure this is what you want to do? We're behind you, but don't sell yourself, um . . . don't let people make a fool out of you." I took their advice to heart, but I went through with it—and I really *liked* it.

One of the best parts is seeing people's reactions. The bachelor is expecting a busty girl with 38D breasts; the bachelorette, a Chippendales guy—they're not expecting me. Actually, one girl, I really thought she was going to have a seizure when I came in; she was shaking. But there's a rule—I call it the Two-Minute

Warning—that for the first two minutes when you see me, you're in shock, you poke fun, you make facial expressions. But after that, I'm just a regular person; the thrill is over.

The guys aren't really that into me, but when I do bachelorette parties it's a whole different ball game: I am the show for the night. The girls think I'm cuddly and cute, and they put dollars down my G-string. We take pictures; we have a lot of fun. And I've gotten offers: They want to see, basically, what I'm packing; they want to know if I measure up to the average guy. And I have to say, I think I do.

> It's all about doing something different. And having little people or a fat mama stripping in front of grown men—that is not something you see every day.

The guys, on the other hand, are not too keen about putting a dollar down a dwarf's pants. Sometimes they can get out of hand if they've already had a few drinks. I'll come in, and they'll say, "Okay, it's time for dwarf-tossing." You know, throw me around or down an alley. And I say, "No, we don't do that. I'm here to hang out and have a few beers, do a little stripping, and talk guy talk." They just want to have some fun with me; I guess it's a macho thing. But I think dwarf-tossing is against the law. And I have all kinds of back problems, so if they were to do something to me, there would be a major lawsuit. So I just strip to my boxers. And the guys crack jokes and we have fun.

Once the female strippers come, they forget about me. And actually, I did one bachelor party with a female little person. And the guys were all over her, throwing dollar bills at her. I was off to the side; they didn't care about me. But they thought she was the greatest thing since sliced bread. She was on the pole and doing crazy stuff, and they just never saw that before from a little person.

I think that's why people hire me: Having a little person at the bachelor party is unique. It's all about doing something different. And having little people or a fat mama stripping in front of grown men—that is not something you see every day.

And I have tons and tons of costumes. A lot of people request mini Elvis and Mini Me; some people want a mini baseball player or a mini drag queen. I was recently hired for a bachelor party at a plumbing company in upstate New York and they wanted me to be a mini Superman. I didn't even strip; I just hung out with the guys and drank beers and talked shit. It was amazing. They paid me a lot of money—because I was there for like ten hours—and I did absolutely nothing. I was taking tip money while I was eating a roast-beef sandwich—it was kind of weird. And the guys were just talking about what kind of year they had, how much money they made. They were cooking hamburgers and chicken. Later on, the girls came in; so again I was basically the opening act.

But I've had a couple of bad experiences at bachelor parties, where the guys got really drunk and followed me to my car and they were saying I didn't do a great job and they wanted their money back. And that is one of the reasons I always, always, always get paid before I start the show.

My base salary is from $150 to $250 for a fifteen-minute show, and my tips could be another $60 to $80, depending on the party. And actually, every time I'm leaving for a bachelorette party, my wife will make a comment like, "Don't forget to flirt with the girls." And my response is, "Listen, you see our child over there? She needs shoes, she needs to go to college. I'm doing it for her." That's my way out. And there is some truth to that; we have a lot of big things coming up: My daughter wants to go to camp, she wants to have her First Communion, she wants nice clothes, she wants an iPod—these things cost money.

The way I see it, this is how God made me; this is who I am. Of course I've had people come up to me and say, "Why do you do this? Why do you lower yourself to stuff like this?" I'm not doing anything illegal; I'm not having sex with anyone; I'm not selling drugs; I'm not doing the dwarf-tossing thing—I'm entertaining people and putting a smile on their faces. I'm using my size to my advantage.

I'm not doing anything that another person wouldn't do in my situation. In fact they're doing other things, like dressing up as elves at Christmastime or as leprechauns on St. Patrick's Day; they're coming out of boxes and surprising people at corporate offices. And some little people have regular jobs, some are still going to school. Everyone is doing their own thing.

I can't make everyone say, "You're doing a great thing." But I enjoy what I am doing and I enjoy making people happy. And you know, I've done pretty well.

Virtual Debate
Strippers Fight Back

It's not just brides venting online. Here's a snippet from stripperweb.com, a site by and for strippers. In this particular forum, the topic was bachelor parties and why brides hate the tradition and the entertainers.

SUBJECT: Brides hate strippers!!

MissIndependent: As some of you know, I just started planning my wedding . . . so I have been spending an ungodly amount of time on wedding websites. I just got into a posting match with a beotch who is talking about how "strippers are whores" and blah blah blah. What started it was a woman asking, "If your fiancé did any of the following at his bachelor party, would you leave him?"

1. WATCHED
2. LICKED WHIPPED CREAM OFF OF VARIOUS PRIVATE PARTS
3. LAP DANCE
4. HER RUBBING BOOBS ON HIM
5. ANY SEXUAL ACTS WHATSOEVER

B-Real: My family owns a bridal shop. And some of these girls—and they are girls—get all excited (which is a relatively mild word) for the wedding itself. They become obsessed that every little thing is perfect, yet they seem like they could care less who the man is standing at the altar. And then these girls wonder why the guy doesn't show up, or goes off with another girl. So MissIndependent, I think you got chatting to one of these brides who doesn't care who their guy is, as long as she looks good in the dress and everything goes according to HER plan.

FancyPants: It kills me the way the blame always falls upon the stripper, but it's the MEN who should get the backlash. Mind you, there are some NASTY strippers out there. I was a topless waitress years ago for stags, and the stuff I saw HORRIFIED me!

Glenda: Like FancyPants said, these women are mad at the wrong people: The problem is the asshole men. The same guys who fool around at their bachelor parties will be diddling their secretaries in five years and boning the babysitter in ten. Do the brides hate secretaries, coworkers, and babysitters? If they suspect they can't trust their man at a bachelor party, for shit's sake, don't marry him.

Foxxi: I have done private bachelor party shows for a long time, and I don't know if I've just had a really good run or what, but I've found that most bachelors are usually pretty well-behaved. There've been a few who have been complete assholes, who have made me think, "Jesus, your poor fiancé."

Heather: I don't even think to myself how this guy is going to be getting married soon. I just think of how I am going to get my money and embarrass the hell out of the groom so his buddies will tip me more.

madmax: I heard of one party where the strippers put chewing gum in the bachelor's scrote hair.

DJ_Star: The best bachelor party prank I ever saw was the group of farm boys who wanted the dancer to let them know when the groom got excited during the lap dance. I figured they were just going to make fun of him or, at worst, take a picture. But when the dancer "noticed" out loud that "somebody was having a good time," four of the BIG farm boys moved in and depantsed (and deboxered) the groom, spread-eagled him, and soaked his erect crotch with John Deere—green spray paint. Seems this is a family tradition!

Free_Spirit: I consider the bachelor party to be a ritual, a place where guys are supposed to let it all hang out as a way to prepare for the commitment of marriage. In no way would I ever hold the actions of a man on this one night against him or judge him as a potential life mate because of it. I could care less what my fella would do at a party. I acknowledge that my views are different from many.

trixi: I give you "props" for having that attitude. Many guys would consider you to be the perfect girlfriend. =) But I'd kill my BF if he crossed the line.

ChicagoJackie: So many men "keep their noses clean" at

bachelor parties, because there's the fear of it getting back to the bride-to-be. I know of one situation where the girl manipulated the groom's best man (by getting him drunk and stoned) to tell her all that went on, and it was a fiasco. The wedding was postponed for three weeks until the fire abated a bit.

GalaxyGirl: I think that most women hate bachelor parties and strippers because of their insecurities within themselves. They are afraid that their fiancé is going to see something in the strippers (self-esteem, fun-loving, "outgoingness"—I think that's a word, LOL) that they do not possess and that their man is going to be attracted by that.

Jane: First let me say that I've been doing bachelor parties for about seven years. It is astonishing to me that I've only danced for maybe five bachelors who *did not* want to touch me. Those five gentlemen will probably stay married. I make bank from bachelor parties. They are fun to do. But I wouldn't marry a guy who wanted a party.

Free_Spirit: I met with one bachelor and his best man to set up their party in advance. While we're talking, the bachelor gets a phone call and hands me the phone and it's his fiancée! She says, "I love your website! You are so cute! I'm so glad you're doing his party! Do you know where I can find a male stripper?" It was one of the funniest things ever.

guest: It's funny, after talking to lots of bachelors on their night out, the ones that say their fiancées sent them off with their blessings are the guys that are the most respectful and least annoying.

Naughtynancy: It's wrong to blame the dancer for the gentleman's indiscretion. However, I've seen bachelor parties at the clubs I've worked at where the groom's friends got him completely wasted and then threw him into the VIP room with the raunchiest girl in the house. A man's general reasoning skills are a little compromised at best. So it's also the friends' fault. I've also seen girls at the clubs reach over the rail to grab the bachelor and shove their tongues down his throat onstage, while the poor guy is struggling to get away. So sometimes the dancers are a little more sexually aggressive than they need to be at a bachelor party.

Ruby: My former husband did in fact cheat on me the night of his bachelor party—not with a dancer, but with the girl that eventually sang at our wedding. So those silly brides are wasting their time worrying about strippers—they need to worry about your average Jane and what she's willing to do. The singles bars are full of girls that will "put out" to just about any guy that pays attention to them and buys them a few drinks.

GoodKitty: The last bachelor party I did, the bride's father told me his daughter sent him to make sure things didn't get "out of control." I told him to reassure his daughter, because I'm not interested in her fiancé—only his money!

THE NAUGHTY CLOWN
Ouchy the Clown

For Ouchy the Clown, a self-described "porn clown" who lives in the Bay Area, it's not about the money. A successful real-estate broker by day, he performs at bachelor parties and events because "it's an outlet for my absurdity and my personality. I'm behind a clown mask and people don't know who the hell I am, so I can be as outrageous or crazy as I want to be."

Ouchy the Clown is a character I created in 2001. He is a professional dominant[6], a disc jockey, and an adult sex clown. What that means is, I *don't* do kids parties.

I get hired by people who think it's gonna be funny to have some weird, half-dressed clown at their party to do what I do, which in those cases is to just walk around and poke and jab at people. Or I get hired to actually go and administer birthday spankings or shavings and that sort of thing.

I've done fifteen, maybe twenty bachelor parties. More often than not, I'm hired by guys in their late twenties, early thirties—urban hipster sorts. I'm not there because I'm "sexy." I'm there for the novelty and humor.

The first bachelor party I can remember was for a friend of a friend, who was not someone I knew. And it was weird because it was like a traditional bachelor party in some hotel with all straight

---

6 professional dominant (n) the person who does the whipping and beating in an S&M session

guys. None of them hired a stripper, but they hired a male adult clown and I was like, "What are you guys thinking? *This* is gonna be your entertainment?" They hired me to beat the bachelor, which I did. The bachelor had never done something like that before and he wasn't quite sure what to think about some large clown pushing him against the wall and beating him. It was silly and fun. And then I drank all their liquor.

They're expecting a stripper, and instead they get a two-hundred-and-twenty-pound male clown.

I'm always nervous about the same thing before a party, that I'm not gonna give them what they're expecting. I don't have a friggin' act; I don't do a stage show. I'm just me, my personality. And it's funny because when I talked to my wife before that first party, I was like, "What am I gonna do?" She was like, "Just do your thing; just be yourself—that's entertaining enough for most people!" And I guess she is probably right.

When I do a party, I show up in makeup and costume. My costume is a leather thong thing—it is called a posing strap—big black leather boots, a simple black leather harness, black satin wrist cuffs, and a black satin neck ruffle. Oh, and a little black satin hat with a pom-pom on it. I also bring a little yellow toolbox. In it I have my razor-sharp claws, nipple clamps, suction devices, noisemakers, hand puppets, clown horns, a couple of pieces of paper with bad jokes, canes, whips, floggers, paddles, an electric-shock device, a couple of rubber chickens, and the sole of an old shoe. Those are my supplies. And balloons and the balloon pump, because I don't have enough lung power to blow them up with my mouth, plus with a balloon pump you can put an uninflated balloon inside someone's orifice and then inflate it.

I come in and make some balloon animals, tell some bad jokes, crack my whip a few times. Then I strip the bachelor and spank him.

Usually, when I arrive, the bachelors don't know what the hell is going on. They're shocked and confused; they're expecting a stripper, and instead they get a two-hundred-and-twenty-pound male clown. So they're like, "What the hell is happening? What have my friends done to me?" So, you know, I come in and make some balloon animals and do some fake juggling (I don't really juggle), tell some bad jokes, crack my whip a few times, mingle with the crowd for ten, fifteen minutes. Then I strip the bachelor and spank him for a good fifteen or twenty till he's red and hurting. It's funny—straight men don't mind showing their asses, they just don't want to show their dicks. And when I beat them, they only show their ass, so they're fine. As it unfolds, they usually go along with it, because what are you gonna do? All your friends are there, and if you don't go along, you're a complete ass.

The most fun I had was actually at a bachelorette party. It was in a wealthy suburb of Palo Alto and they were all really young, like twenty-two to twenty-five. Normally what happens, like at a bachelor party, is I ask, "Okay, who wants a straight-razor shave?" And everyone is like, "Ha, ha, ha—that's really funny." And they change the subject. These girls, I brought out the straight razor and I shaved seven women's pussies at that party. It was like, "Me next! Me next!" And I'm dripping wax on them, putting needles in their nipples. I had a real hoot, because they were *so* into it.

I still do Ouchy at bachelor parties and events, but I don't get contacted as much anymore. Maybe the novelty has worn off.

THE PAINTBALLER
Roy J.

Roy J. is a fifty-one-year-old paintball park owner from Iowa and a devout Christian. He's seen his fair share of bachelor parties, and he has some pretty strong opinions about the ritual.

We're getting more and more bachelor parties. I don't know if it's the fact that paintball is getting more popular or if our park is getting better known. But I don't know where all the bachelorettes are at. I think the girls are kind of afraid of paintball; it might be a little too much for them because it stings when the paintball hits—and it leaves a welt.

> I think most bachelor parties are not worth going to—unless you're into drugs and drinking and watchin' whores dance.

I think guys like the competitiveness. It's the old cowboys-and-Indians routine: one group against the other. But they are definitely out to get the bachelor a little bit more; they all seem to aim their guns at him.

Sometimes the group comes before the regular bachelor party. If they come after, usually a few of them don't feel like playing much; they are a little hungover. But once they get to playing, it kind of changes; once they get the adrenaline pumping, they really get into it. Still, I would have to say that the Christian bachelor parties are the best ones to have out here. They come clear-eyed;

you can tell they ain't been out drinking the night before.

Personally, I think most bachelor parties are not worth going to—unless you're into drugs and drinking and watchin' whores dance; that is what a bachelor party is to a lot of people. But you know, it shouldn't be; it should just really be something where you want to get together with your friends for the last time, you know, and go bowling or paintballing or whatever. But the drinking and the having other women around before you get married, there is just something ironic about that. But, you know, the world is not as wholesome as it used to be. . . . So are ya married? You got a family?

A fair question—that I did my best to avoid fully answering. While I didn't disclose my sexuality, I did explain to Roy that, after talking to dozens and dozens of people about bachelor parties and hearing about their married lives, I find the institution a little scary and unrealistic. And a week in Vegas, America's quickie-wedding capital, only confirmed my theory.

Chapter 4

What Happens in Vegas . . .

WITH CHEAP AIRFARES, LAX LAWS, AND A NAUGHTY, come-hither ad campaign, it's not surprising that Las Vegas hosts tens of thousands of bachelor partiers each year—not to mention more than one hundred thousand weddings. Taking the "booze + strippers = fun" equation to the next level, the Vegas bachelor party has become the epitome of the ritual, a male status symbol on par with the ladies' two-carat engagement ring.

Truly understanding today's bachelor party requires spending some time in Sin City, seeing the parties in action, and talking to the locals who make it happen. I arrived for a six-day stay with the goal of chatting up as many bartenders and cocktail waitresses, taxicab drivers, bellhops, and twenty-four-hour wedding-chapel managers that I could muster the nerve to approach. I also brought along two

willing (and hetero) friends, Lenny and Craig, to assist with
this research and pose as my wingmen.

THE WEDDING PLANNERS
Anne S. & Jennifer H.

Anne S. and Jennifer H. are young, single wedding planners in
the Venetian Weddings Department. With little prodding, the
sassy, power-suited duo launched into an energetic dialogue
about the Vegas wedding business and the challenges of search-
ing for mates of their own in a town crawling with guys who,
according to Anne, "are here for the weekend for a bachelor
party, just looking for their weekend fuck."

Jennifer: We do fifteen hundred weddings a year here. We have three
different locations: the gondola, the bridge over the Grand Canal,
and the chapel. On a busy Saturday, we'll have twenty-five or thirty
ceremonies. Like Valentine's Day two years ago, we did thirty-six!

Anne: The more I do these weddings, the more it changes my per-
ceptions of people and relationships. There are couples that you
see and you're like, "Wow, that's what I aspire to have," but there
are other couples where you think, "What are you doing? Why are
you getting married?"

Jennifer: I had a bride a couple of weeks ago who just did *not* like
her fiancé! He went to kiss her at the end, and she wouldn't. And

I'm thinking, "That's so messed up!" It's sad to see so many couples planning their wedding, and I'm like, "Why are you making it into such a negative moment?"

And I've had a lot of people cancel. I had a couple come all the way from England with their families. And the bride didn't show up for her hair appointment the day of her wedding. So I called her room and the groom answered. I told him and he sounded surprised and said, "Okay, I'll try to track her down and have her call you." An hour later, one of their parents called and said they weren't going to get married; she was having reservations.

I've had probably three or four cancel after they got to Vegas because something happened here. One was canceled because the groom went out the night before for his bachelor party and cheated on his fiancée. She called me, bawling, "I'm not marrying that S.O.B." They ended up coming back two months later and getting married. She was like, "I should have known better than to bring him to Las Vegas." And I'm thinking, "That's crazy! If you can't trust him here, you can't trust him anywhere."

Anne: We see it all. We have a lot of mail-order brides. We have one couple we're working with right now—and she's marrying her ex-husband's brother.

Jennifer: I've had people who got married here, got divorced, and are getting married here again.

Anne: There are *some* sweet stories, like the couple who dated in high school, separated, were married to other people for twenty years, had kids—and I think maybe their spouses died. Then they met each other again randomly at a business conference, started talking again, and eventually got married out here.

Jennifer: You know, they should totally make a reality show about us! We could have our personal lives incorporated into it. . . .

Anne: Yeah, *The Venetian Wedding Planners.* There are some crazy stories.

Jennifer: Oh my gosh, I have the worst story. At every rehearsal, I say, "Go out. Have a good time tonight. If you drink, please be careful." Well, I had a groom who got alcohol poisoning. First they had to postpone the wedding for an hour and a half, but he was still too sick. So the paramedics went up to his room and gave him an IV drip. He was really dehydrated and puking, but he still wanted to get married and she did too—even though *I* wouldn't have wanted to marry him. So we had to go up to the suite and perform the ceremony there. Right after that, the paramedics took him to the hospital. I've also had a couple of drunk brides. One was staggering out of control down the aisle. And our ministers typically won't perform ceremonies if they know the couple is really messed up. But for some reason this one did; maybe he didn't know. There's been a couple of times on the canals where the gondolas have said, "We're not taking them," because it's on the water and they can't have them be that crazy.

Anne: It's not just people being drunk; it's every single aspect of the weddings. We've had mothers try to cancel them for their kids and people try to crash ceremonies.

Jennifer: We sometimes have passwords for brides and grooms, so only they can get information about the wedding. Because one time, we had an ex-girlfriend call and cancel. She knew their address, she knew their phone numbers, and obviously she knew their names, so she pretended to be the bride and canceled everything. Then the real bride called to check in, and I was like, "You canceled it."

My first year in Vegas was not so great. Then I came here to work and it's been really, really good, because I have a good job and sometimes you get to meet cool people. But Vegas is a weird place. It's really transient and the dating scene is dismal. I mean, I'll be in a club or just out and about, and I constantly hear the rowdiest guys and they're like, "He's getting married!" And they're doing the nastiest things.

But even the people you meet at local bars are weird. Like I went out to dinner with a guy, and we're sitting there, and he takes his teeth out and puts them on the *table*! And he's like, "I used to box and got my teeth knocked out and I can't eat well with them." Okay, well then don't take me out to dinner on the first date!

Anne: I recently went on a double date. The guy was really nice. And I was like, "Oh my God, is it possible that he's normal?" So we go back to his house for a drink and there are knights everywhere, and swords and statues and shields and crap on the walls. I felt like I walked into a Medieval Knights Tournament at the freakin' Excalibur. I'll go out on a date and it will take me a good three or four months to recover before I say, "Okay, I'll try this again."

THE RAT PACK
The Bachelor, Nathan S., Amir T., & Felix C.

Because I sensed that a gay guy with a tape recorder wouldn't exactly be ushered into the party, I enlisted two straight friends, Lenny and Craig, to help me infiltrate a bachelor party at the relatively tony Bellagio. In fact it was Craig who spotted a group of about a dozen guys at the hotel pool. "Over there," he said. "That's a bachelor party. Trust me." I engaged them in a bit of guy talk about poolside booze service—and then went in for the kill: "So are you guys here for a bachelor party?" Craig was right; they were on day two, trying to recuperate from night one. While the bachelor was reluctant to talk, his mostly married—and totally buzzed—friends, especially Nathan S., Amir T., and Felix C., were eager to discuss their Vegas exploits, past and future.

Felix: Really, the weekend has nothing to do with the bachelor. It has everything to do with us, the guys who are already married. I'm telling you, that's what it's all about.

Nathan: I've been married a few years. It's wonderful; I love it. But it's just . . . I remember at my bachelor party, what I was willing to do. I was like, "Oh my God, do I even want to touch her tits?" Versus now, it's completely different. The difference is, she had my balls then. After a few years of marriage, you settle into things. You can relax a little bit; the newness wears away, so you can be a little more wild.

Amir: And you look forward to your friends having bachelor parties.

Nathan: This time, we're here for two days. We got in last night. We went to Tao for a while. Some of these guys dropped a C-note to get into the club, and then we had table service,[1] which was really expensive. Then we went to Deja Vu, a strip club. I have no idea where it is—a taxi took us off the Strip somewhere. And that was good. There was no alcohol, but it was nice.

You gotta understand, a stripper's not a real girl.

Felix: Girls, E tabs,[2] and Vegas. Done. There is nothing in life that is better than feeling a woman's breasts when you are rolling[3] on ecstasy. Hypothetically, you can do that anytime. The only thing is the wives and girlfriends; you can't just be like, "I want a guys' weekend to go out and do all these things." It's the ritual of "My buddy's getting married, we've got to send him off in style." And they buy in to that. Because it's a bachelor party, they can't say no. They probably think we're having a harmless weekend; they think we're just having lap dances and that's it. The line is here—and we're just going slightly

1 **table service** (n) getting a table at a nightclub by guaranteeing to buy a certain amount of booze, aka bottle service
2 **E tabs** (n) Ecstasy tablets, also known as MDMA; a synthetic drug that induces an ecstatic feeling, but may also deplete brain cells
3 **rolling** (v) *slang*, using, having fun, tripping

over it, but not *way* over it. Really it's just a question of money. If I had a little bit more . . .

The Bachelor: I don't know. I wouldn't, like, go over the line; I wouldn't have sex with a stripper.

Amir: I think he will. Dude, alcohol takes away all sense of responsibility.

Felix: Yeah, I think he will. But I don't want to know about it.

Nathan: But you gotta understand, a stripper's not a real girl. You know, if I catch my wife with a neighbor, that's a problem. But a stripper? I think what women are afraid of is that men are going to leave them on an emotional level for a stripper; that we're going to find a girl who is better than them. But all we really want is tits and ass.

That's the way I think we need to start looking at these things. A few thousand years ago in Pompeii, they had whorehouses on every block. It was just thought of as men having certain needs and they get it done and then they come home and that's it. I mean, if my wife went to a male strip joint and I heard she danced with a guy—that would be fine, because it's all physical.

Felix: There is of course one very important rule: Never pay a stripper more than twenty dollars for a dance if you can't touch her. I'd be glad to pay forty or fifty or whatever, but then I want to touch. I also say, "Watch a girl give a dance to another guy first." A lot of times they'll look really hot, but then I'll get a dance and it will be one of those weak dances. Honestly I spend more time thinking about this stuff than I do actually working. You should see the e-mailing that goes on beforehand. Do you know how excited we've been for the last three weeks for this thing?

Nathan: He passed out, by the way, at Tao—in the club—and security asked us to take him home.

Felix: It's not as bad as our other friend who threw up in the strip club.

Amir: And in the taxi.

Nathan: Wait till you see us tonight—we will be on fire. We're going to Marrakesh for dinner. Then the Circle Bar at the Hard Rock and to Sapphire's for the VIP rooms. The bachelor's a little green; he didn't do E last night, but he might tonight. It'll be a great experience. The first time you do it is easily the best. It's all down-hill from there; you can never relive the first time.

Felix: To make it even more interesting, he's marrying a Muslim girl. It's gonna be this big religious thing. This will be the last time he can indulge in anything that's nice. It's all over for you!

The Bachelor: Her parents are very constricting.

Nathan: We're gonna hurt this boy tonight! Pretty much it's just gonna be each of us kicking in seventy-five bucks—there's eight of us—and getting a girl. Put him in the VIP room for forty-five minutes and whatever happens, happens. I know the way he is; he probably won't do much at all. Or we could have two girls back in the room. That's the big debate: Do you go to the strip club or do you actually get women sent to the hotel room?

Amir: Have you ever seen these cards for strippers that they hand out on the Strip? I did it once. It's a total rip-off! The girls that show up aren't the girls on the card. They charge you ninety-nine bucks just for showing up. And then they come in and they show you their tits and that's like an extra three hundred bucks. And if you want anything after that, you gotta negotiate.

Felix: Once they get your money, they do whatever they do for like ten minutes and then say, "If we don't get more money right now we're gonna leave." And they have you by the balls at that point. It's a bad experience. That's why we're *not* going to do it tonight. If it turns out shitty then it's fucked; we have one shot. It's feast or famine.

Nathan: As you can tell, this is not our first bachelor party in Vegas. We did mine, and we did another one of our friend's before that. And then we'll have Amir's sometime next year. Vegas is the best place in the world for a bachelor party. Tons of strip clubs, beautiful women, usually very good weather, gambling— everything in the world you could want.

Felix: I brought five thousand dollars. The reality will hit Monday morning. I always want to say, "I'll never do Vegas again," after a weekend here. But if you *don't* do weekends like this, then what the fuck's the point?

E-mails from a Best Man: Part One

From: Jay
Subject: Noah's Bachelor Party
Date: Aug 2, 2006 7:16 PM

Yes, gentleman . . . it's hard to believe and bittersweet, but Noah is in fact due to face his day of reckoning this fall. How can we commemorate the end of such a lifetime of blissful bachelorhood? VEGAS, BABY! VEGAS!

SAVE THESE DATES: October 6-9th (Columbus Day weekend)

GAME PLAN:
Fri, Oct 6: Arrival & Warm-Up
Sat, Oct 7: The Main Event
Sun, Oct 8: Recovery, aka more mischief

DETAILS, DETAILS:
1. Hotel: Rates for Luxor are going for $200-220/night that weekend; plan to double up and save some dough.
2. Late-Night Entertainment: LV Bachelor Party offers VIP shuttle and club access for $150/pp/night. Plenty of cash machines and $1 bill cashiers abound.
3. Gambling: Bring only what you're prepared to lose.

I will get back to you with more details as plans unfurl.

Cheers,
Jay, aka "The Best Man"

Money does seem to have a different value in Vegas. People who haggle for a twenty-dollar discount on a vacuum cleaner back home are suddenly shoving said twenties into slot machines and G-strings. But it's not really about money—it's about the status and the access it can buy: to guest-only pools, the hottest nightclubs, the sexiest strippers. Clearly Nathan, Amir, Felix, and company have learned how to navigate—and how much cash to bring—through trial and error. But what about most guys, who are showing up for the first time? That's where VIP party-planning companies come in. They specialize in organizing stag weekends for out-of-towners.

THE VIP HOSTESS
Natasha K.

Natasha K., a striking Wyoming native in her early twenties, came to Vegas to go-go dance but ended up in the club-promotions business and now works as a party host for one of the bigger VIP players. We met up at the Mirage, and in a relatively quiet corner of the casino she offered her take on the festivities, her clients, and her adopted hometown.

I've hosted every kind of bachelor party. The first party I did was like nineteen Chinese guys. I've taken out a group of guys in their seventies who were having a bachelor party for a second wedding. I had a group of cops. I had a group of doctors who were all on Ecstasy the whole time. They were trying to tell me, "No, it's okay. I've done my research and it's fine." I had one party where the bachelor kept switching. The first night one guy was like, "I am the bachelor." And the next night, he was like, "I'm not the bachelor. *He's* the bachelor," because they were all doing bad things, so they didn't want me to know who the bachelor was.

You see, when people come to Vegas they become like a different person. People who wouldn't normally do drugs are rolling the entire time—asking for coke left and right, drinking the entire time. For three days, they're fucked up and they don't give a shit. They're living the celebrity rock-star life. That's what you come to Vegas to do. But the thing is, if you want to go to a club here and you don't know somebody at the door, you're not going to get in. Especially if you're a big group of guys.

[The company I work for] has established relationships with every club in Vegas. We know the doormen and are able to take parties and walk them right into the nightclub. They don't have to worry about getting there and holding their dicks in line and being like, "We can't get in." I see that all the time. And if those guys do get in, it's going to be crowded and they're not going to have a place to all hang out together.

With us, we arrange table and bottle service, and you can have your own roped-off VIP area with security guards and cocktail waitresses. So once you're in the nightclub, you feel special, like you're somebody. And because you prepay us, you don't feel like you're paying for anything. I pay for the limos, the gratuities for the person serving the table. And I order the bottles and pay for them. So you feel VIP the entire night.

What a lot of guys don't realize is that I'm there to walk them into the clubs; I'm not there to be their private entertainer. And a lot of times they'll look to me to set the mood. But I can't *make* them have fun—that's up to them. Sometimes you have a group of guys just sitting there and it's boring. I'll try to get a party started either by trying to get them drunk quicker or by bringing girls over.

What I'll often do is go around the club and pick out girls and say, "Hey, ladies, want to come drink for free? I'm with this group of really cool guys." And I'll bring these hot girls to sit at the table. There's also this guy named Shorty—he's a dwarf or a midget—and sometimes he'll come out with the bachelor parties. And he is *so* much fun. He'll pull girls over like crazy, and they're all, "Oh, he's so cute." He just grabs their hands and brings them to the table. And they'll even out the ratio—or we'll have even more girls than guys! That's what really makes the party: having girls there. The girls are the ones to get all crazy and dance and show their panties and kiss the bachelor.

When you break it down, I'm just an overpaid babysitter. Usually the guys are good in the beginning; they're all hyped up and ready to go. I make sure that they all get out of the limo and get into the club and, you know, we don't lose anybody. And when we go to the next spot, I make sure that they're all together and, basically if anything goes wrong or if anybody's too drunk, that they get back to their room.

There can be a lot of drama. There have been groups that get really out of control and wind up getting kicked out *after* spending like six thousand dollars, because one guy is harassing the cocktail waitress, putting his hand on her. I had one guy end up in jail for doing drugs in the bathroom at Rain at the Palms. I tell guys ahead of time, do not do drugs in the club. But that happens quite a bit. Let's see, I had guys who had strippers come to their room who stole their money. I've had bachelor parties come down here and make plans, but the night before they gambled all their money and lost everything and couldn't afford to party.

When people come to Vegas they become like a different person. They're fucked up and living the celebrity rock-star life.

It's kind of ridiculous, the amount of money people spend. Let's say the average size group is ten. They usually stay three days and spend at least ten grand—a grand each for partying and eating and going out. That usually doesn't include the hotel or airfare. People always try to save money, but they end up spending it anyway.

I think if you really want to have a good time in Vegas for three days, you should budget three thousand dollars. It's a lot of money, but for three days you're living like an absolute rock star.

You're living like Ben Affleck or something. And that includes your alcohol, your gambling, your dining, your entertainment, your whatever. Sometimes guys will plan a golf day, but they'll be too hungover to make it. Anything you plan for the day in Las Vegas, especially if you have a long night, probably won't happen.

That's the thing—it becomes almost a competition of who can outlast who. One group recently, I dropped three guys off at an Asian massage parlor at nine in the morning after a night of partying, you know, to get their "happy ending." They were the only three out of a bachelor party of fifteen that lasted. They tipped me like six hundred bucks.

I work off tips. No, I'm not gonna hook up with a guy, but the more I kind of tease, the more money I'm going to get. I try to give them all equal attention, but you can always pick out the one guy who has the money. You can't tell initially, but there is always one guy who's paying for all his buddies.

And yes, I've had bachelors try to get with me. One of them said, "I'm only getting married because my family is part Indian, and if you're not married by the time you're twenty-nine, you're considered gay." And so he's trying to hook up with me and I'm just like, no.

If I was getting married and my fiancé was having his bachelor party in Vegas, I would probably have my bachelorette party here at the same time. That way I could keep a better eye out and he would know that I'm here and wouldn't feel like he could do anything, because you really can get away with anything in this town.

E-mails from a Best Man: Part Two

Subject: Noah's Bachelor Party: Budget
Date: Sept 28, 2006 4:55 PM

BUDGET:
Estimate about $1,000 beyond the costs of flights and hotel. (Of course, it depends on how many lap dances you'll need.)

250 Meals

120 Clubs

300 Strip cash

110 Mountain biking

75 Limo

150 In-room entertainment

1000 TOTAL

I apologize if the plans seem too expensive. I want to make sure that you have realistic information on what our mischief might cost.

Also, for Saturday night's commemoration of Noah's bachelorhood, please come up with answers to the following:

1. Grossest moment you've experienced with Noah

2. Example of how Noah is a dawg

3. How you know Noah's gay (e.g., he loves to wear spandex
unitards)

See you fellow ne'er-do-wells soon!

THE NIGHT CLUB BOUNCER
Alton G.

It was difficult getting locals to go on-record (or return my cold calls). Thankfully, Natasha opened her Rolodex, providing names and introductions to others in the business, including Alton G., a bouncer at two clubs popularized by MTV's *Real World Las Vegas*. Alton knows firsthand what happens on the other side of the velvet rope. And, protected by confidentiality, he talked freely about the "crazy shit" he's seen and what Vegas bouncers really think about bachelor parties.

I work the front door, so I'm the first one to hear the stories, like, "Hey dude, there's ten of us. It's my buddy's bachelor party and we want to come in."

Hopefully, for their sake, they've called in advance to make table and bottle reservations—or to just get on the list.

A lot of times bachelor parties come to town and they're like, "Yeah, I'm going to hit this, I'm going to hit that, and we are just gonna go wherever." They don't see that they're just one of many, that we already have like six other bachelor parties at the club. Just know that with any bachelor party, you have to be patient with the bouncer, and don't come with the attitude and ego, like, "My friend owns a company and he's getting married. It's his time," because everybody is somebody in Vegas.

The management terrorizes us, like, "If you take money, you will get fired." But if a guy wants to get past the line, it's usually twice cover.

Unfortunately I have to say no all of the time, because we have to maintain the integrity of the club. There is a certain girl-to-guy ratio. If there are too many females, although it looks really nice, females ain't the ones that buy the drinks; they just don't. Guys have the ego, so they buy the bottle and they're just going to spend more. But if there are too many guys, well, that's just self-explanatory: Nobody wants a cockfest. And then guys get cranky, because everyone's talking to the same waitress. Of course, if they're high-rollers and they got money then, you know, anything is possible.

And anyone can work a deal. A lot of the clubs try to keep a hold on that, but they realize that it's Vegas and it just kinda happens. The management terrorizes us, like, "If you take money, you *will* get fired." But if a guy wants to get past the line, it's usually twice cover. So if the cover is twenty-five dollars, then it's fifty dollars to get past the line, and he still has to pay the cover charge. And once he gets in, it's going to be expensive. If it's ten guys, you're looking at a three-bottle minimum at three hundred fifty dollars a bottle. But if we're busy and you are not on the list, it's not a sure thing. And if it's guest-list only, it's guest-list only.

More often than not, the guys just don't have a plan. Or the limo driver just drops them off here. They planned transportation, but they didn't plan ahead with the clubs! Sometimes the limo driver can talk to the main host and he'll take care of them and get the ten guys in. But even that's not guaranteed.

That's why you call VIP companies like Natasha's and all those cats. They can set things up. They have a partnership with the club's director of guest services and can negotiate a set fee. So we would take a bachelor party from a VIP company versus your ragtag group of bachelor guys that just walks up, because, you know, they always bring people that are going to spend money, that are going to buy bottles. It's already prearranged.

Have you ever had to throw out a group of bachelors?

Absolutely. Sometimes they just get too crazy. Usually it's not the whole group. It's one or two guys who think, *Dude, it would be cool to do my girl on the balcony of the VIP area; let me see if I can get away with that.* They do it because it looks cool or, you know, shows off their status. And then they'll have a story, like, "When we got married, you won't believe what Tim got away with!"

It's craziness, the stuff people pull, like going in the corner and peeing. *Dude, the bathroom is right there!* I've also caught bachelors doing lines [of coke] and stuff on the table—just right in the open. It's not cool. And that's where I come in. The party's over; they have to leave.

When people are drunk and they're just about to get married, they vent, and it makes the people around them realize where their life's at. I see that all of the time. It just all starts coming out, you know. And the bachelors are just trying to get their last hurrahs; they want to do something that they probably won't be able to get away with once they get married.

You know, we get hookers in the club all of the time; I call them my worker bees. One was telling me that, bachelor party-wise, she'll get guys that have wanted to do something their entire lives: a fantasy—or some latent sexual urge or something. But when it comes down to it, he'll be like, "Oh, what am I doing?" And at the last moment he won't do it.

But I think it's perfectly okay—you ain't married yet! Have at it. Don't have that nagging regret. I tell my friends, "I'm getting this all out of my system now." That way I don't have those urges later, and have a midlife crisis when I'm forty-five.

THE STRIP CLUB MANAGER
Lola R.

Lola R. is a friend of a friend in Vegas and a cocktail manager at one of the most popular gentlemen's clubs in the city. Fresh from a day of second grade, her seven-year-old Heather tagged along for the interview. At first I was a little worried that Lola might censor herself in front of her kid, but she assured me that her daughter had heard it all. And so, as Heather worked quietly on her mathematics homework, Lola told me what she's seen behind the curtains of one strip club's legendary VIP rooms.

I came by way of California and Dallas. I started out in strip clubs when I was twenty-two. I'm thirty-two now, so it's been a while.

I think that people get a lot crazier when they come to Vegas; they feel a lot more free, like what happens here doesn't count. When I worked at clubs in California and Dallas, it was a lot more composed; the people didn't get as nutty.

Ironically, the nuttiest thing I've seen actually happened in Dallas. I was upstairs in the dressing room and this dancer came running in and she had blood all over her, and she was freaking out. Long story short, she was going down on a dude in a bachelor party—and they were both on something—and she bit down and severed the vein underneath. Blood was everywhere, and the guy would not get in the ambulance because he didn't want his wife to find out. He was like, "She's gonna divorce me; she didn't want me to come tonight." I've always wondered how he explained *that*.

Now I'm the cocktail manager at a club here in Vegas. I work in a VIP area, which are private booths that have curtains completely

around them. I've walked in on all different levels of undress. And
when people say there's no sex in these rooms, well, they either
haven't spent enough money or they haven't met a stripper that's
good enough at hiding it.

There are obviously certain customers that you kind of look the
other way for. When I don't know a customer, usually the dancers
are very discreet, but I've been in the business long enough that I
know what they're doing. Of course, if it's in your face and we walk
in on some girl going down on a dude, it's gonna get stopped, and
that dancer's gonna get fired.

I've probably seen more than five hundred bachelor parties.
We get so many at this club, it's just ridiculous. I don't really like
them. Not to sound shallow, but at this point, being in Vegas for
the past three years, I've seen the amount of money that goes
through this town—and bachelor parties just don't spend the kind
of money that other people do! They're on a budget in a big way,
but they want the VIP treatment. And dancers avoid bachelor parties like the plague. A lot of the time, everybody buys one dance for
the bachelor. But dancers do not like doing twenty-dollar dances;
our girls are spoiled. You say, "Can I get a lap dance?" And they say,
"You wanna go for three for a hundred in the VIP room?" That's
three dances for a hundred dollars. And if you say no, they're like,
"I'm busy." And they'll walk away. Because, like on Saturday night,
we had a regular come in with some friends and they each had two
strippers. That night he spent $21,000 just on the strippers.

On the other hand, for the average bachelor party of ten guys, a
very average group of guys from Middle America, I would say their
bar tab would usually be about seven, eight hundred dollars. Maybe
they'll spend another two grand on dancers. That's very, very, very

middle of the road. And it kills me, because I think about it: It's four hundred an hour in the VIP area. Most of the guys that are coming in from Iowa, Missouri, and Oklahoma—they don't make that in a week. But they're happily willing to give up four hundred for an hour of a girl's time.

My personal opinion is that these are the girls they feel are just out of their league. These are the girls they've fanatisized about from high school and even now. And on any given night they can pick and choose and find that girl who is their dream girl physically. As far as personality goes, a good dancer will become the girl you want too. And these guys come in and they'll stay for like seven, eight, nine hours. They really get sucked into it here.

I think there are some men who really, truly would rather go golfing or go on a rafting trip with their buddies for their bachelor parties. But it's rare. When bachelors first get here, they all say, "I don't really go to strip clubs," and, "I'm only here because my friends made me come." I can't tell you how many times a night I hear that. A few shots down the road and all of a sudden they're professionals. They're getting dances, they're going into private areas, and it's a whole different story. I think that they really mean it when they're sober, but when you drink, your inhibitions go away and you want to have fun and party.

The younger guys are always really gung-ho from the second they step into the place. And when you get a big group of young guys, like early twenties, the average mentality goes down to about age thirteen. And that's when you start having problems. It's always the end of the night, and they don't want to pay. They say, "Those dancers weren't good enough; I'm not paying for it." Or, "I didn't order twenty shots." I love it when we have a group of twenty guys and they dispute the bar tab. They're like, "We didn't drink eight hundred dollars worth of liquor." And I'm like, "Are you kidding me? There's twenty of you. One round alone is going to be close to two hundred." They're drunk, so they don't remember. Luckily there is always that one sober person in the group who's like, "Seriously, we did drink that much." There's always that voice of reason.

I think there are some men who really, truly would rather go golfing or go on a rafting trip with their buddies for their bachelor parties. But it's rare.

The older guys, they're the ones who are usually like, "I'm not too sure. I don't really want to get any dances." They always end up in the private areas because they're not really comfortable with what they're doing, but they do want to do it. The funniest thing, we had this one bachelor party—it wasn't very big, only about eight guys—but it was the guy getting married, his dad and grandfather, *and* his father-in-law-to-be and his grandfather-in-law-to-be. They all ended up in a VIP booth. And I walked back there and I'm watching grandpa feel up a stripper. I was like, "Are you kidding? Isn't this just a little weird? Does anybody else have a problem with it?"

It's funny, because I see that a lot: The father-in-law will be at the bachelor party and he's getting lap dances right alongside the groom. But that was the weirdest one, because it was both the dads and both the grandfathers. I really think it's that whole male-bonding, loyalty thing. And it's like your acceptance into the family. But I wouldn't be able to sit next to my mother-in-law and get a lap dance.

I am actually divorced. I was pretty young when I got married. My whole thing was, "You're going to have strippers, that's cool. But if I find out you slept with them, the wedding's off." I don't think I would react that way now. But I was way too young, which is why we divorced. I tried to do the whole controlling, no-strippers-and-you-can't-do-this-and-you-can't-do-that routine. But it all went on. They ended up having four strippers, got a hotel room, games were played. And everything else that I said I didn't want to happen, happened. I think there's nothing that you can do to prevent it. No matter what the groom says, his friends are still gonna do it. There isn't a friend in the world who loves him enough to forego a bachelor party.

Ultimately, I do think bachelor parties are worse in Vegas because you have that ad campaign: "What happens in Vegas, stays in Vegas." People forget that some of us actually live here, and have lives and kids and families. And being a woman in Vegas, people automatically think you are a prostitute. I'm propositioned constantly.

By day four, I was physically exhausted and had pretty much heard enough. I spent most of my remaining time in town in the

hotel's spa—steaming, napping, and soaking. In a Jacuzzi the size of most suburban backyard swimming pools, I met a dashing gentleman with a French-Canadian accent. With all this "guys gone wild" talk, I decided I needed to get mine and invited him up to my room. As we were fooling around, we swapped bios. When I told him about the book and my research, he laughed. Turns out he was married with two kids. And why was he in town? For a bachelor party, of course! Only in Vegas . . .

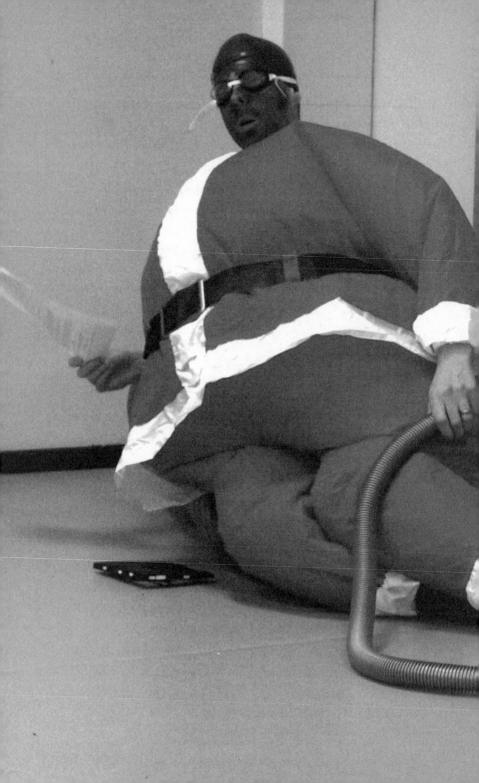

Chapter 5

And Now for Something Completely Different

EVEN AS SOME MEN GO EMO[1] AND MORE WOMEN GO bridezilla, the stereotypically smutty bachelor party remains the norm. Minus the shoulder pads and big hair, it looks a lot like Tom Hanks's celluloid *Bachelor Party* back in the eighties— and every popular imagining since.

As with most stereotypes, there's some truth to the last-fling free-for-all, but obviously it's not the whole truth. In reality, some bachelor parties are drug-soaked, others are prayer-filled. Some are glitzy Vegas affairs, others so casual they're indistinguishable from any other night at the corner bar. What they all have in common is that, in different ways, each is a reflection of the bachelor, as well as his family and friends.

....

1 emo (adj) *abbr* emotional; often used to describe an emotionally driven subgenre of punk rock

THE HIPPIE BACHELOR
Cade H.

Cade H. was raised in Woodstock, New York, and the twenty-nine-year-old admits he's a product of his environment. "In many ways, Woodstock lives up to its reputation as a haven of free thought and all the stereotypes you have about hippies." Growing up, Cade had a core group of friends whose families were similar—their parents were children of the sixties and somewhat countercultural. "So it was not surprising that we would have fairly unconventional weddings and bachelor parties," he explains. "And the traditional bachelor party—where you need to have your last fling before you are trapped into marriage—seems pretty outdated."

I was the first of this group to get married. And when my friends started planning something for me, it was pretty obvious we were not going to do the strippers and gambling in Atlantic City kind of thing. For us, doing something like that would have been so demoralizing, because we consider ourselves a creative group of guys, who are always trying to do cool things together, like Burning Man.[2] The only reason to do something like hiring a bunch of strippers would have been because it was completely unexpected. In fact, they did joke with me, like, "Oh, we're going to go to the 'Legs and Eggs' breakfast at the Foxy Lady in Providence. It'll be crazy." Obviously I knew it was a total crock.

....

2 **Burning Man** (n) a weeklong art and music festival held every year in the Nevada desert; the event's motto: "No spectators!"

Going into it, all I knew was that it was going to be a long weekend on the East Coast, and it was not going to involve any women. They also told me to bring clothes heavy enough to be in the elements. So I figured we were going to do some kind of camping, because we're all country boys.

I opened my eyes, and on the mantle was an architectural drawing; it took me a second to figure out what it was.

They picked me up in New York City and just said, "We're heading north." We got off the highway at the Woodstock exit. My folks still live there and they have about forty acres of land, and there is nothing on it except for a tiny cabin. We drove to this cabin, and when we arrived they actually blindfolded me. And this was the only part that was a surprise: We went into the cabin and they positioned me in front of the fireplace. I opened my eyes, and on the mantle was an architectural drawing; it took me a second to figure out what it was. I was like, "These are trees, that looks like a bridge." And I looked around the cabin and there were tools everywhere, and it all came together: "Oh, it's a treehouse!"

Now, we are all a pretty handy crew—and one of my best

buddies is an architect—but of the ten guys there, this is definitely not everyone's idea of a great time. But they know I love to build stuff, and for a while I was obsessed with this book about treehouses. So they knew I was going to love doing this. And it was totally fantastic!

The next morning, we hit the ground running. We spent three and a half days up in the trees, putting this treehouse together. And when I say treehouse, I don't mean like a little kid's treehouse. It is basically a ten-by-ten-by-ten cabin with a huge deck, two doors, functioning windows, and retractable steps to climb up. It is fully sided, fully insulated, with hardwood flooring and wood paneling.

At one point, I think on the Saturday night, one of my friends was like, "Cade, I'm sorry we didn't really get drunk." And then he asked, "Does anyone have any dirty stories about Cade?" And we sat around the campfire for about five minutes while people were like, "Hmm. There was that time when you got drunk and hit on my sister." And that was as naughty as it got. The cool thing is, it wasn't just about that weekend; it's a gift that I'm going to be able to use whenever I want to. (At least until the building inspectors find it and make me take it down.)

That weekend was so much fun, it inspired us. And the next time one of our buddies got married, we tried to one-up my weekend. For Rom's party, we went through the same kind of process: What does Rom love to do? Now Rom happens to be very competitive and he's the most athletic of us all. So we decided to have a weekend of competitions, to basically divide the bachelor party into two groups and have what we called the Rom Challenge. Because my friends had done such a good job for me, there was a fair amount of anxiety about living up to that, and I knew if I didn't do for Rom what he had done for me, I was going to feel really shitty. But it all turned out great.

Now we're on our third one, and it's getting really out of hand. I bet this happens to other groups of guys, too, where the first one has a really fun bachelor party and then he feels like, "Oh, I have to pay them back for how much fun that was." And it snowballs, and they get more and more of whatever they do.

So the third one is coming up July Fourth weekend. My friend Jonah is getting married and the weekend is called The Jonanza. We've plotted out a Choose Your Own Adventure[3] map of Northern California. We have all of these intersections where we can go left or right, north or south, starting at the Golden Gate Bridge. And we have researched the hell out of what is going on in Northern California that weekend, including a rodeo in Folsom, the Napa County Fair with a pie-eating contest, archery classes and go-karts, cool little caves, and a great winery that has a crazy back room—all these things that we could be dropping into. We could never do them all in a weekend, but they are all along the different routes.

Throughout all of this, we're going to be filming it, and then we're going to splice it together into a movie to show at his wedding. And again, part of what is so fun about it is that the whole thing is very reflective of Jonah's personality.

And the next one after that? Who knows who is going to get married next—but I'm sure the bachelor party will be equally silly and crazy. If we just take whoever it is to Vegas and get him laid, I think he would feel pretty shitty. So we'll really have to step it up.

....

3 **Choose Your Own Adventure** (n) a popular children's book format from the eighties that's made a campy comeback

BOYS ON FILM: THE SEQUEL

Guys looking for inspiration and a new twist on the traditional bachelor party aren't going to find it on Netflix. Instead, they'll find mostly recycled clunkers, a few scattered chuckles, and an Oscar nod or two.

Bachelor Party (1984)

Date with an Angel (1987)

The Simpsons, "Homer's Night Out" (1989;

Season 1, Disc 2)

House Party 3 (1994)

Stag (1997)

Very Bad Things (1998)

A Guy Thing (2003)

Sideways (2004)

Bachelor Party 2 (in development)

THE ADVENTURE PLANNER
Darren H.

Darren H., a Detroit native, believes most men are not exactly like Cade and his friends. "I'm relying on the fact that guys don't plan anything." That's one of the reasons the twenty-nine-year-old founded Adventure Bachelor Party, which arranges all kinds of outdoorsy and semiextreme sports trips for the groom and his pals.

Three years ago, I started getting an itch to start my own company. One night I was sitting at a bar with my brother, brainstorming ideas. We talked about running transportation between bars as kind of a trolley system, because so many people were getting DUIs. And that kind of evolved into bachelor party transportation. Then it kind of went into, "What about organizing adventure bachelor parties?" In the back of my mind was an article from *Maxim* that talked about this new trend in bachelor parties—about deep-sea fishing and cattle wrangling, and it listed the various vendors that did each thing.

Bachelor parties are an ideal business for a few reasons: People have discretionary income and are willing to spend it because "it's a bachelor party" and guys kind of go all-out for it. Also, I knew that women are not big supporters of Vegas and strippers, which is the traditional bachelor-party market.

I haven't been married, but I am pretty sure this is how it works: The woman's planning this wedding and is very high-strung, so the man has to be as accommodating as possible. And when it comes to the bachelor party, the groom has to figure out, "How can I can I keep her happy, but also keep my friends happy? How can I have a bachelor party that she will actually support?"

I figured if I were to create a service and actually sell it to the bride and the wedding coordinators as a "clean" version of the bachelor party, with enough excitement and adventure to it that the guys wouldn't be turned off by it, then I could have much more of a mass-market appeal.

Now I'm booking about a trip a day. Usually it's the best man calling. About 10 percent of the time it's the best man's girlfriend or the bride herself looking to help with the bachelor party. I also have mothers and fathers calling me. Yesterday a sixty-five-year-old lady called me about her son. It was just like a sitcom. She yelled to her son upstairs to come down and talk to me about bachelor party ideas. The grooms are actually calling a lot more, saying, "These guys are lazy. I just want to get something going, because I want to do something cool. And they all want to go to Vegas." I've probably had that exact conversation twenty times.

How did you choose what activities to offer?

There are a bunch of variables. It can't be something that guys are comfortable planning, because then they don't need me. So it's not going to be a hunting trip, because anyone that enjoys hunting, plans hunting trips. Another thing is, it needs to be an adventure, but it can't be *too* adventurous. I originally had mountain climbing on there, with repelling and all that, but it just limits my market. To go out and sit in a raft or go fishing is an adventure, but you could be thirty pounds overweight and still do it. Whereas for sky diving, there's a limit: You have to be under 230 pounds. So there's a subtle line: adventure, but nothing that requires you to be in extreme shape. The third variable is, Is this something that a non-experienced person could do right out of the gate? I was going to look at doing fly-fishing, but that's not something you can just walk out into a river and start doing. The same with surfing.

When it comes to the bachelor party, the groom has to figure out, "How can I keep [my fiancée] happy, but also keep my friends happy?"

We don't include strippers in our packages, because basically that would eliminate my whole theme and most of my PR. But there's a little bit of smoke and mirrors going on, because everyone who contacts me wants to know if there're strippers. And the things on my checklist when I'm determining where to send guys are: Do they have strip joints? Do they have casinos? How far away are they? Because everyone asks me. It's one of those things where, if they find out or I slip them some information about where the strip joints are, then so be it. But I don't promote it.

Darren sends guys from Manhattan to ranches in Texas, and groups from Chicago to seaside communities in Florida. For those willing to spend the money, where one resides need not limit the bachelor party. But before the birth of the "destination bachelor party," and for those still on a tight budget, the party may be shaped by the groom's locale and the regional flava.

THE DEEP-FRIED STAG
Clark S.

Clark S. grew up in Virginia, went to Vanderbilt University in Tennessee, and attended his first bachelor party more than two decades ago in small-town Alabama. "Basically it was a *Hee Haw* version of what I expected," explained Clark at the beginning of our phone conversation. He then retreated to a more private spot in his home, "so my wife won't hear all this stuff."

A friend of mine who I had lived with my senior year, was marrying his high-school girlfriend right after college. They're from a rural area, near a town called Luverne, which is out in the middle of nowhere. They were the cream of the crop in their little world: She was the smartest, most beautiful, most interesting woman in the town. And he was the smartest guy, and all those things. I think people at home expected him to marry her.

Most of the guys at this bachelor party were from college, guys from Chicago and St. Louis and Dallas and Atlanta who were from money. There were also some of his local friends, who were impressed with the Vandy[4] crowd and saying, "We are in high cotton now." That means we are among important people. So it was a bunch of hicks and a bunch of rich kids, and there was a little bit of friction.

The bachelor party was the night before the wedding. We went to this hunting lodge on a man-made pond. We started drinking and eating deer meat. (Somebody had killed a deer and cooked it whole; it covered this entire picnic table.) Then these two chunky prostitutes came to the house, which was essentially a log cabin. They looked like the people on the *Jerry Springer Show*; they were wearing cutoffs and tube tops. One was blond and one was brunette, and they were both probably about thirty-five years old. And these whores were very ugly, but they were probably the only two whores in town. You know, if this town of five thousand had *three* whores, I would be surprised.

There were no airs put on. They weren't dressed up nice or anything—they were just there to do a job. And it was surreal. They danced on a tabletop to ELO's greatest hits on vinyl, and I thought it was hilarious when they played "Evil Woman." Then we realized that one of the country guys was a virgin, even though he was probably twenty-one, twenty-two years old. So this Gomer Pyle[5]–ish dude was serviced by these whores, who were shocked to find out that he had an enormous penis. We watched the whole thing. There was a firewood pile outside the

....

4 **Vandy** (n) *abbr* Vanderbilt University

5 **Gomer Pyle** (n) a Southern simpleton portrayed by Jim Nabors on *The Andy Griffith Show* and its Gomer-centric spin-off

window and we crawled up on top of it to look in.

The groom was also serviced by them. I think his attitude was, "I'm just getting a simultaneous blow job from them, so it doesn't count." And I think he had a special dispensation to do it anyway from his fiancée. I have some sympathy for him, because he was like cattle being led down a chute. This was his last moment of freedom, the only wild moment he was going to have. In that regard, I understand it, because he was definitely going into a very conventional, obedient life. He was permitted this outlet and he took it.

They were wearing cutoffs and tube tops. And these whores were very ugly, but they were probably they only two whores in town.

After the whores finished, I got into a boat with a friend of mine. It must have been about three or four in the morning. I was very drunk, and we had both taken mushrooms[6] and were not ready to go to sleep. So we get on this boat and we see there are cows really close to the edge of the water. All of a sudden, as I am turning around

---

6 mushrooms (n) natural hallucinogenics, also known as "'shrooms"

looking at these cows, I am slammed across the boat into my friend. We had run full-speed into a barbed-wire fence—it was running across the bottom of this cow pond—and they've got the fence electrified to keep the cows from running into the water and drowning.

So I go to the emergency room—high on mushrooms—in Luverne, Alabama, with blood pouring out of one of my eyes and my back. And this is big excitement in Luverne, that people from the city are spewing blood everywhere. And for about ten years after that, I had a scar in the shape of a cross on my back that was about a foot long and blue—one of those raised scars—and a scar above my eye. The whole thing was sort of a deep-fried version of a clichéd bachelor party.

I went to the wedding the next day with a bandage wrapped around my head and a black eye and stuff. All the talk was about what happened to us; that sort of overwhelmed everything, because I was pretty seriously hurt. But I showed up anyway and I looked pretty scary. Now I wish I had a picture of myself in a suit with the black eye and a bandage.

The bookend of that tale is, twenty years later I went to a bachelor party for a friend who works at a magazine. It was me and three other guys. Everybody at the table was a journalist, a longtime New Yorker, and over forty—and one guy was over fifty. We went to Sparks[7] and had steaks. And we were home by eleven o'clock. That was the middle-aged version of whores, drugs, ELO, and voyeuristic sex.

....

7 **Sparks** (n) a famous New York steakhouse, where mob boss Paul Castellano was gunned down in 1985

THE MORMON BACHELOR
Bryce C.

Much like geography and age, sometimes religion dictates what does and does not happen at a bachelor party. "Scriptures, testimonies, and root beer are the staples of the traditional . . . Latter-day Saints bachelor party,"[8] wrote Todd Hollingshead in the online newspaper of Brigham Young University. Still, a drunken naughty bash remains the point of reference even for the pious.

"We don't drink and, theoretically, we don't have sex until we're married," explains Bryce C., a practicing Mormon in Southern California. "So that kind of eliminates two aspects of stereotypical bachelor parties." His party, with his non-Mormon, D&D-playing, punk-rock-loving friends from high school, was anything but typical. But it wasn't particularly Mormon, either.

I was actually the only Mormon at my bachelor party. I consider myself fairly religious, so I never imagined a Vegas weekend with the guys. But I wouldn't have been offended or minded if there'd been a stripper; I would have thought it was funny and rolled with it. My only fear is that I would have been cornered alone in a room with her, and then I would have looked dumb and had to tell her, "Sorry." You know, thanks but no thanks. But

8 Hollingshead, Todd. 2003. "Mormon Bachelor Parties Break Traditional Mold." *BYU NewsNet*, January 22.

I don't think most of my friends that were there would have been comfortable with it either. It would have been uncharacteristic for the group.

We were kind of the gamers in high school. We would play Dungeons & Dragons or other strategy games pretty much every weekend. We weren't socially inept, but most of us didn't really get into the whole dating thing. A couple of us had girlfriends, but for the most part it was "bros before hos." Even though my friends weren't Mormon, we shared similar values. I guess it just ended up that way.

Our friend David was always the Dungeon Master. I have known him since kindergarten, so I asked him to be my best man. For old time's sake, a bunch of us had gotten together around that time to play some D&D. And we all had a really good time. So I said that it would be cool to get together and do something like that again for my bachelor party. David was really excited about that idea and ran with it. So we got together for a weekend and we pulled out our old D&D characters and I think we even ran an old adventure. My character is a mixed-class character; he's a Dwarf Fighter/Theif named Domax. It makes us sound like total nerds, I know, but Dave is actually in a fairly well-known punk band.

The party was heavy on the nostalgia. In a lot of ways, nothing had changed: We were laughing at the same stupid jokes and playing the same games, and the same dynamics of the group were there.

It was kind of the last hurrah—at least on my end. I know it makes it sound like marriage is this sudden imprisonment, but it's one of those things you are told so much: "When you get married, things are going to change, and it will never be the same." And it might just be that I was buying into that. But there is this fear that it won't be the same—that, even if we do it again, my wife might call and say, "Our daughter is sick," or something.

And Mormons regard marriage as something really sacred—not that other religions don't, but it has certain ramifications in the afterlife. Generally, if you get married in the Mormon temple, it is for eternity, not just until death do you part.

THE BORN-AGAIN BEST MAN
Peter M.

Some men do choose to make religion, prayer, and testimonies an explicit part of the bachelor party. Others, even the most religious, choose a more secular approach that may be at odds with their scriptures.

Peter M., a preacher's son, grew up in the church. As the pastor that runs the Men's Ministry at the Midwestern megachurch helmed by this father, Peter is sometimes asked for advice about bachelor parties. He tends to quote two pieces of scripture: "Bad company corrupts good morals" (Corinthians 15:33), and "The spirit is indeed willing, but the flesh is weak" (Matthew 26:41). Explains the pastor, "If it compromises your morals, you need to get out of there."

I didn't have a bachelor party when I got married nine years ago. I didn't need one. I had been dating my teenage sweetheart for five years; I couldn't wait to get married. I was twenty-one and I was a virgin; I chose that. I didn't need a bachelor party to remind me what I was leaving—I couldn't wait to leave it, man. I mean, my friends couldn't give me what she could give me.

That's the thing about the Christian bachelor party: You remember what you've done and you don't have to worry about telling people what you did.

My cousin was a little bit of a late bloomer. He didn't get married until he was twenty-eight. And I planned his bachelor party. I wanted to do something that was special for him. I didn't study the whole bachelor party thing. I just began to think, "How do you throw a bachelor party for a guy who believes in God?"

I decided to center the entire party around what he likes, obviously not from a carnal standpoint. My cousin likes to eat, so we took him to a Japanese steakhouse. He loves to golf, so we took him golfing. He loves movies, so we rented his three favorites. He likes to play cards—this is maybe where you get into a gray area—so we took him to a casino for an hour and a half.

We started at two o'clock in the afternoon and got done at three o'clock in the morning; it was a thirteen-hour event. He thought he was just coming over for a regular afternoon out with me, but I surprised him. I'd made calls to all his buddies from his hometown, and they all came up and were down in the basement hiding when he arrived. After about thirty minutes of talking and celebrating and letting the surprise wear off, I said, "Well, bud, we have a two thirty tee time and we need to get on that." So I centered the entire day around the friends, the food, the fun, and the fellowship-type deal.

The fact that I took him to a casino was a big deal. For text-studied Christians, obviously there's no gambling. But I wasn't trying to be religious and I wasn't trying to be legalistic and predictable. That's one thing that always drives me nuts: when you have Christians that get together and everything's got to be a scripture, three points and a poem.[9] Just have fun for a change! And that's why I did it for him.

We didn't pray together before we went. We didn't say, "Lord protect us, keep us safe and strong. May we not do anything unwise or unfit." We just said, "Hey, we are going to have a blast. We have already planned out the entire day." And I was saying in my heart, *I trust the Lord that it will go as planned and as I intended.* And it was just a fun day with his most favorite people, and he'll never forget it.

That's the thing about the Christian bachelor party: You remember what you've done and you don't have to worry about telling people what you did. There was no drinking or carnal or questionable activity involved. I think the clichéd bachelor party

9 three points and a poem (n) a once-popular structure for Christian sermons in America, especially the South; of late, preaching has moved in a more narrative direction

is very disappointing. I don't see what's enjoyable about getting a person you call a friend all liquored up, wasting your money, and watching him consume something—that being alcohol, that being a lady, that being a lap dance—the night or the weekend before he's getting married.

You can say the same thing about us going to the casino. Maybe mediocrity ruled. But I put together the party so quickly that I didn't have time to bring in a dealer and say, "Let's play with Oreos," or something goofy or cheesy. So I thought, *Maybe going this one time won't hurt us.*

On the way to the casino, I did pray. I said, "Lord, I know this is something you don't approve of, but just for this section of time, it would be great to be profitable." Now you could say that He answered my prayer, because I made nine hundred dollars. But the problem is I don't agree with gambling at casinos; I went just to have fun with my cousin. And I haven't gone back since.

THE BEACHY BACHELOR
Mark G.

For San Franciscan Mark G., the decision to skip the strippers and head to a beach in Costa Rica had nothing to do with morals. "I had done the Vegas thing and the stripper thing, and everything in between. And I have nothing against strip bars," he explains. "But I figured if everyone's going to spend five hundred dollars, why not make it a real memory that we can enjoy together and actually talk about?" For men over thirty, after indulging in a half dozen nearly identical outings, it gets a little

tedious. Faced with the prospect of another hedonistic blowout, some men settle on an appropriately expensive dinner-drinks-bed-by-midnight routine. Others, like Mark, who wed at thirty-six, choose to pursue a much grander course of action.

All my friends basically grew up in the water, surfing. And our hearts are in the water. My wedding happened to be in Costa Rica and my friends were all going down there for that, so I suggested we head down a week early and go camping and surfing. I threw it out there and nobody hesitated; it was just go, go, go. In all honesty, I think most guys sign up for those canned bachelor parties with strippers because they don't see other options—and it is probably the easier way to go. To get a group of guys to Costa Rica, there's effort involved. But most of the crew I run with are pretty self-sufficient; they don't need their hands held.

We camped up near the Nicaraguan border, and it's probably one of my favorite places in the world. It's basically off the grid: You need four-wheel drive to get there and you've got to bring all your own gear. I mean, just going to get more beer and ice would be a ten-hour adventure. So once you're there, you're there, versus a typical bachelor party, which is very produced and a paid experience. It's X amount of dollars, and at this time this is going to happen, at this time we're gonna go here, and then, you know, there's a grand finale at two in the morning with one or two strippers. And then usually the group breaks apart.

The area we went to is a pretty raw place with a lot of wildlife and seven of the most poisonous snakes in the world. It gave the whole experience an edge. It was kind of *Mosquito Coast* meets *Lord of the Flies*. I gave all the guys machetes—that was my gift to them—so there were a few excursions out in the woods, running amok and trying to fight off this local type of raccoon that was trying to attack us.

Our real goal was to get in the water and be surfing as much as possible. And during the walk down to where we were surfing someone was always offering me advice. About half the group is married, so they're telling me, "Marriage doesn't change anything." The other half said, "Man, it is going to change so much. Get prepared."

In the end, we totally pulled it off. Nobody got hurt. We had our ice and beer throughout the trip. And in the back of my head, I was thinking, "We can do this every two years, every five years." It can become, in essence, its own ritual. And it doesn't have to be just about me, it can become an "us thing."

BROADWAY BACHELOR

Tony Award–winning musical *The Drowsy Chaperone* began as a series of skits performed at a bachelor party for actor Bob Martin. Not wanting the coed bash to get too racy, he requested there be no strippers. To entertain the crowd, his friends Lisa Lambert, Don McKellar, and Greg Morrison created a parody of a 1920s musical about an over-the-top wedding, which featured characters based on the happy couple. Eight years later, Martin starred as himself alongside Sutton Foster when the show was mounted as a full-scale production. The rest is Broadway history.

THE GAY BACHELOR
Will B.

After a few thousand years of bachelor parties, the desire to do something, *anything* different makes a lot of sense. But for gay men, bachelor parties are a new frontier. Gays have long influenced the culture at large. Exhibit A: musical theater; exhibit B: media-savvy activism; exhibit C: real estate values of once-deserted neighborhoods. Now that marriage for same-sex couples is legal in many Western countries—and civil unions are gaining acceptance in the United States—I wondered if the "gay bachelor party" could provide clues to the future of all bachelor parties. For the moment, that seems unlikely. According to several Provincetown wedding planners and an unscientific polling of gay and lesbian friends, most queer folk seem to be ditching the prewedding ritual altogether. Not Will B., a thirty-seven-year-old writer and artist.

My husband, Josh, and I had separate bachelor parties. At first he said, "Maybe we should have one together," because we have a lot of the same friends. B ut it was our last night of bachelorhood. And if we did it together, we would have worried about the other person—or maybe not be as zany or as crazy as we were.

Things got a little tense before the parties, because some of Josh's friends were like, "What are you doing for *your* bachelor party?" And my friends were like, "We're not telling."

I thought it was going to be just four or five of our friends getting together and drinking. The only thing I said beforehand was that I didn't want to be too embarrassed. Of course, that was shot straight to hell once we had a couple of drinks.

I kissed like twenty men that night. It wasn't like I set out to kiss everybody—it was part of one of the games we played. Whenever someone said congratulations, I had to kiss someone. And we had like kazoos and penis straws at the restaurant. There was a point where I had a candy jockstrap on, and people were taking bites of it. I also wore a veil with little penises on it to the bars. And people were really great. They were cheering and clapping, and patting me on the back.

When we got on the subway, there was actually a group of women who were out shopping for a friend's bachelorette party. They thought we were a straight bachelor party. So at first, they were like, "Oh, when are you getting married and what is she—your fiancée—like?" But within a few minutes they realized, and they were laughing hysterically. They also had like this eleven-inch dildo they had bought for their friend, so they were taking photos with it and with us. And we had a sing-along on the subway. I think we sang "Going to the Chapel."

One of my closest friends from college was at my bachelor party and he is straight. He went to all the gay bars with us and we tongue kissed—or touched tongues. He had a ball. He was like, "I can't believe how much fun I'm having. It's just like the other bachelor party I went to, except that party had strippers."

I had never been to a bachelor party before, but mine had meaning. It was a celebration of my friends. And it was fun to take the traditional bachelor party and turn it on its ear. We mocked it, but at the same time enjoyed it. It was all my closest "girlfriends" getting together and sending me off. We were making fun of my "last night of freedom." Because ultimately Josh and I still have a lot of freedom, because we

Infamous Bachelor Parties:
ELTON JOHN AND DAVID FURNISH, 2005

Topless waiters wearing black ties and riding boots. **Elizabeth Hurley**. **Ozzy Osbourne**. And a video message from **Bill Clinton**. Sir Elton and his filmmaker hubby made headlines with their star-studded stag party in London. The couple made it official on the first day civil partnerships became legal in England and Wales, with a civil service at Windsor's Guildhall, the very place **Prince Charles** married **Camilla** just months earlier. Touché!

are in an open relationship.[10] So the bachelor party isn't too different from what Josh and I could do out on our own—or together. We had a "don't ask, don't tell" policy about our bachelor parties—unless there was something we wanted to share with each other.

I actually did hook up with a friend of mine at my party. It was something we had both flirted with for a long time, but we were like, "No, we are friends. We are not going to let this happen." It was really nice and great fun, and I don't regret it at all. I think it was kind of my last grasp at something, because if we hadn't had the bachelor party, that probably wouldn't have happened. So maybe the party was an excuse for it to happen.

I chose not to share it with Josh, because I didn't want to give him anything to worry about. The weeks before getting married

....

10 open relationship (n) a nonmonogamous relationship

were such an emotional and stressful time. I probably should have told him, but my first instinct when I got home the next day was to be like, "Oh, I crashed . . . I just passed out." Of course, that's what he said after his bachelor party. . . .

Did you always think you were going to get married?

No. And that was in my vows. I said, "If someone had said to me six years ago that I would be marrying the guy across from me in the lecture hall, I would never have believed it. But here I am."

I certainly was thinking long-term from almost the beginning, because I am older than Josh and I was ready to settle down. But that did not include marriage. I'm not against it, but for me, settling down means living with someone and committing myself to someone emotionally. And that is really all I wanted.

I was not expecting him to propose at all. In fact the evening we were celebrating his getting into graduate school, I said, "If you need to go away and go to school for a few months, then maybe I could join you afterward. Whatever you need to do, I support you." And he said, "I'm glad you brought that up, because there's something I've been wanting to ask you." And I was like, "You are not going to ask me to marry you, are you?" And he said, "Yes, I am." And he pulled two rings out of his pocket and said, "I am not going to go away to school unless you go with me. So I am asking you right now, will you marry me?" It completely threw me, but it was a validation of his love for me, because I think I was a little insecure before that about what he felt for me.

I think we wanted to do the wedding, because we wanted to do something creative and have fun. But for me, it was also one way for my family to see the wonderful people I surround myself with. My father is a former cop and FBI agent. I came out when I was eighteen—now I'm thirty-six—and it has taken a long time for my dad to come around. He has gotten a lot better, as far as asking me about boyfriends or who I'm dating, but he only met Josh for the first time when he came for the wedding. And my stepmother told me he was very nervous about coming. You know, he had never hung around with a bunch of gay people.

It was all my closest "girlfriends" getting together and sending me off.

I don't know what happened, but he completely turned around. Actually, after the wedding rehearsal we went to a gay bar, and we kept trying to talk my dad into going back to the hotel, like, "Aren't you tired?" And he is like, "No, I'm fine." And as we are walking in the door, he jokes, "If you see me start to leave with a guy, stop me." So then I'm playing pool with some friends, and I see this big, buff, bearded guy walk over to him, sit down, and start a conversation. And they talked for like an hour. They were talking about guns and war, of course. But afterward my dad was like, "What a nice guy! That was really a great conversation."

The rest of the weekend he was just amazing. He had a good time, he was affectionate, and he signed our wedding guestbook with something like "I love you guys. I am always going to be here for you." The handwriting was a little shaky, so I assume he was either a little tipsy or emotional. I think he saw that we're not so different from anybody else, that we are actually pretty normal. And I think a lot of his fears were laid to rest. Whether he agrees or not with the way I find that happiness, he wants me to be happy. And I think he saw so much happiness that weekend.

Ultimately, I think my marriage is not so different from my sisters' marriages. It is a lot of other things besides what is on a piece of paper. It's a marriage of minds and bodies and property. And you should see our apartment: We have Crate & Barrel gift boxes all over the place from our wedding registry. And we have rings from Tiffany's—one of the cheapest kinds they had, but still, they're from Tiffany's.

THE SURPRISE BACHELOR
Ronan M.

Some parties are calibrated to the groom's passions and wishes, but many, it seems, go out of their way to humiliate him. It's like a ceremonial way of ejecting him from the tribe for betraying his bachelorhood. One classic prank is dropping a drunken bridegroom in another town, with or without his clothes, and definitely without any money. Ronan M. had a different but equally unpleasant experience in 2002. "You have to remember," the Brooklynite warns me in advance, "I was totally stoned when this happened."

I was at my music studio in Williamsburg,[11] working on a track with my friend. We finished and decided to go back to my apartment to listen to it. We get there and he pulls out this joint. And he never, never, never has weed. So we smoked it and I keep passing it to him, and he totally did a Clinton: He wasn't really smoking at all.

So I smoked almost the entire joint and got totally and insanely high. We're listening to this track and his phone rings. He was dating this crazy Russian that was manipulating him to try to get her a green card, and he is like, "It's Anna. I have to go meet her."

So he leaves, and I'm like, "Okay, what am I going to do now?" A couple of minutes go by and another friend, Carson, calls and is like, "I need to ask you a favor. I found this couch and I got it all the way to my apartment, but now it's stuck in the front door." I tell him I'm coming right over, and he says, "I'm double parked, so I'll just come over and get you."

There was this section of Williamsburg—now there are probably like condos and stuff—but it was a bit desolate a few years ago. We're driving through, and there is this weird dude leaning up against a pole. He is a big white guy. And as we get closer to him Carson slows down a little. This guy stumbles out into the street and he is *bleeding*.

He comes to my side of the car and is banging on the window saying, "Help me!" And I'm like, "Let's get the fuck out of here!" But Carson stops the car and opens up his door and asks, "Dude, are you okay?" And he is like *ugh* and he gets in the backseat of the car!

I'm ready to get out of the car and I don't understand why Carson is not yelling at this guy. But I can't leave my buddy with this crazy person, so I decide to stay. And Carson is talking to him. "Are you okay? What happened?" The guy is like, "My boyfriend stabbed me," and he is holding his belly and there is blood all over him.

Apparently, when they were originally planning it, they were going to hold me up at gunpoint.

So Carson says, "Do you have health insurance?" And he says, "Do I look like I fucking have health insurance?" Now he is lying down in the back of the car, and Carson announces, "We're going to take you to Bellevue." And I am like, "This is what an ambulance is for. I'm calling 911!" Carson grabs my phone and says, "No, he doesn't have health insurance. It is going to cost him all his money." And this guy is moaning in the back. And Carson is running stop signs and red lights. And there are all these cars honking their horns at us. Crazy.

Instead of facing the front of the car, I decided to sit at a ninety-degree angle to keep an eye on this guy and on Carson and on the road, all at the same time. I look in the backseat and notice the guy has his hand in his fucking pants. And I'm thinking, *This is so sick. Dude is going to like, fucking mug us, or he is whacking off.* I'm trying to send Carson a signal, and the guy keeps saying all this weird shit about bums, and all these weirdo non sequiturs. So I say out loud, "I have a really bad feeling about this." And Carson says, "What are we going to do? We have to take him to the hospital." And I say, "We are *not* going into Manhattan. If we are going to take him to a hospital, let's take him to the one near us."

At this point, we're getting really close to the Williamsburg Bridge, and I am totally afraid this guy is going to kill us. And he starts shivering, and Carson's saying, "It's going to be okay." All of a sudden we're on the bridge. It's rush hour, totally gridlocked, and I'm like, "What the fuck are you doing?" He says, "Oh, I just got confused." Great—we are stuck on the bridge with this crazy fucking asshole. So I turn to Carson and I am really having a panic attack. And Carson turns to me and says, "Welcome to your bachelor party!"

The guy in the backseat totally breaks character and sits up. I look at my window, and what I thought was blood was just jelly or something; I had totally been duped. And I was furious. All adrenaline. I quit smoking like a month or two earlier, and Carson is like, "Do you want a cigarette?" And I'm like, "Fuck you, man. Fuck off. Fuck you. This is so fucked up." My whole body was in shock.

I'm sure my friend Brock did most of the organizing. He is an artist, and part of his art is this kidnapping business. He is constantly organizing these things for clients: They pay money and he provides them with an extreme experience. So he knows all these fucking weirdo people.

The only person that really has a deep conscience in that group is Carson, and he was the one that really made the trick work. He felt extremely guilty, because he saw my fear. And it was serious. I thought I was going to die.

I really had no idea it was going to happen, because I never felt like I needed a bachelor party and I didn't ask for one. Apparently, when they were originally planning it, they were going to hold me up at gunpoint. Thank fucking God someone said, "You can't do that. He may jump out of the car while it's moving."

I wasn't psyched for the experience while it was happening, but I was fine with it in the end. I told my fiancée, my parents, everybody—because it is a funny story. I've been to crazier bachelor parties that were much more fun than mine, but the stories weren't nearly as good.

In reality, most bachelor parties are considered a success if they yield a good story and a few compromising moments that can be brought up at inopportune times over the course of a lifetime. My friends still talk about the young couple that showed up, totally lost, during our buddy's stag weekend. The couple stayed for a drink and then started kissing each other. That eventually led to heavy petting and a live sex show. Unbeknownst to the crowd, two of the guys had arranged the whole thing, starting with a posting on Craigslist.[12]

Situations like these seem rooted in the desire to go one better and manufacture an appropriately memorable send-off. Most of these incidents were totally optional and largely avoidable. But, as you'll see in the next chapter, not everybody has that luxury.

----

12 Craigslist (n) a global network of more than 300 urban online communities, each featuring free local classified ads and forums

Chapter 6

We Have a Situation

WHEN TWO INCOMPATIBLE REALITIES—LIKE A SEXY policewoman and an out-of-control bachelor party—collide, there're usually no good options, just varying degrees of discomfort and misunderstanding.

The bachelor party presents a perfect storm for particularly charged moments: There's outsized expectations, there's peer pressure to prove one's machismo, and there's that convenient—if unspoken—oath of secrecy.

But there's also the social reality that "regretfully declining" an invitation is likely to offend the groom-to-be. How else can we understand why some sticky situations are not avoided all together?

THE FATHER OF THE BRIDE
Saul S.

It's hard to imagine why the father of the bride would accept an invitation to his son-in-law's bash. That's what I hoped to find out when I talked to Saul S., who attended his son-in-law Rick's bachelor party in 2004.

I had never been to one. When my wife and I got married in 1970, we spent thirty-five dollars on our wedding—not this $200,000 that affluent people are spending now. It was a whole different time: You were starting off absolutely penniless. You had to work to put food on the table, so we weren't really thinking about bachelor parties. We got married on a Friday, and I was back at work on Sunday.

I was totally surprised when I got a call from Rick's best man and he told me I was invited. I was thrilled and honored, but a little anxious: I am thirty years older than these kids, and you hear what goes on with these parties. So initially I felt that maybe it was *not* appropriate for me to be there. Then I found out the groom's father was invited as well, and I felt a little more comfortable. I also realized that, knowing my prospective son-in-law and my daughter, it would be reasonably clean fun.

I did talk to my daughter before going. I think she had complete confidence in what was going to go on—that we wouldn't be stepping over the edge. The only thing she said was, "I hope you get enough sleep, Dad."

The bachelor party was held in Vegas. I really didn't know what the agenda was, except that they were planning a surprise for Saturday night. We all checked in to the hotel Friday afternoon. All the guys began to get together, and we greeted one another and had a cup of coffee or a beer. It was a feeling-out period—finding out what they all did for a living, their educational status. By Friday evening, the wall basically came down.

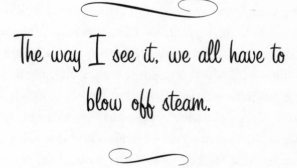

The way I see it, we all have to blow off steam.

That night we went to a noisy restaurant, a fun place with lots of energy, lots of people, and a lot of drinking. Afterward, I think the guys stayed out until about four a.m. drinking and carousing— and I went to sleep.

The next night, Saturday, we all went out for a really wonder-ful dinner at one of the major steak houses. We finished around twelve thirty, and then a couple of cars came and took us to a place called Crazy Horse 2.

I had never been to a place with lap dances and strippers, and it was an absolute riot. Rick's father, who is a couple of years older than me, turned crimson red, as did I, and the kids were looking at us and really cracking up. One of them hired a girl to go lap dance all over us. And they grabbed Rick and got him up on the stage with the strippers, and the whole place went crazy. As this is happening, his father and I are trying to blend in with the back wall, and actually made our escape around two thirty. I don't know how long the rest of them stayed there. But I do know that as I got up for breakfast around nine thirty or ten, a whole bunch of them were just coming in.

The way I see it, we all have to blow off steam. As long as we're all willing participants and no one is getting hurt, I have no problem with it. No harm, no foul. The thing that I worry about, being the father of three daughters and seeing the way women are treated around the world, is that stripping seems so terribly degrading. Yes, these gals were making a living, but I worry that it's leading to prostitution, drugs, and a life less productive than the life they may want to lead. That was my take on it. But I kept that to myself.

I thought Rick handled himself very well; he did nothing that I would have not expected from him. If something had happened that I thought was inappropriate—unless there was some criminal activity—I would have just finished up the weekend and probably had a chat with him a week or two later—you know, let it blow over—because we all do things that we may or may not be proud of.

On the other hand, I would have had a real heart-to-heart with my daughter, which we have done all our lives, and been completely honest. With your son-in-law or daughter-in-law you have to be on a very narrow edge; you really can't discipline them, because they're just getting to know you. You could literally wind up losing your daughter if there was bad blood between the two of you. But you can let your son-in-law know what you think is appropriate.

Fortunately none of that was necessary. Everybody had a wonderful time, and when the wedding came, it was like Old Home

Week.[1] At different points, the guys would go into another room and toast Rick; there was a camaraderie at the wedding that we wouldn't have otherwise felt.

So the bachelor party was a wonderful way to get to know these guys in a very concentrated period of time. And you're setting up a role that's more than just the father-in-law ideal. It puts you, in a sense, with everybody else; we were just a bunch of guys, enjoying each other and having a good time. And I'm really glad I went.

THE SON OF THE GROOM
Jack B.

Being at a son-in-law's stag is one thing, but a son at a bachelor party for his soon-to-be-remarried father—that seems to contradict the natural order. That's what happened to Jack B., who grew up with a commodities-trading dad and his librarian mom. "They're both very nice, very interesting people, but completely different: She's very intellectual and very sweet," says Jack. "And because she is pretty strong-willed in her own way, she definitely restrained my father for many years. But he needed to just sort of do his own thing." Jack's parents eventually divorced. And when he was twenty-five, he had the opportunity to take part in his fifty-four-year-old father's bachelor party.

1 **Old Home Week** (n) To encourage former residents to return to New Hampshire and help fix up their struggling, neglected hometowns, Governor Frank Rollins initiated this official state holiday in 1900. The idea spread and it is still celebrated, with picnics and parades, in towns across New England and parts of Canada.

The thing is, my father was always more like an older brother. For instance, I remember I was seventeen and we were at a club in New York and he was like, "Hey, I think you should have this." He handed me a joint, and now the two of us smoke weed together regularly and hang out, and he hangs out with my friends—they all think he's awesome.

So my father is what you'd call a character. On the one hand, he speaks French and German fluently and went to boarding school in Switzerland. On the other hand, he's a pretty serious biker and he's got tattoos and piercings. He mostly listens to Led Zeppelin and the Rolling Stones, and he likes to get hammered.

I guess the whole time he was married to my mom, he kept his crazier side under wraps. I know they stuck it out for my sake, but they really didn't mesh too well. After they separated, my father immediately moved in with his girlfriend. And this bachelor party was for that wedding.

It was at one of those steak houses that are mostly for businessmen with expense accounts; we rented out a back room. It was about thirty guys—mostly friends of his from work. But some friends that he hadn't seen for ages also showed up. The median age was somewhere between his and mine.

So we had a meal and we're just sitting around this huge square table and drinking. Then this stripper showed up with some burly guy carrying a boom box. I remember she had black hair and was very Slavic looking. And there was a bit of a ruckus, because the guys who had taken care of the entertainment had been very adamant that they wanted a blonde.

There was some kind of negotiation going on. And then this

guy just put on the boom box and played C+C Music Factory or some crap like that. As I recall the stripper was bottomless, and she went around dancing and giving everybody a lap dance. I kind of passed on it.

> Eveybody was egging my dad on. So he lay down on some chairs. And the stripper literally was grinding it down on his face.

I was sitting right next to my dad. Looking back on it now, that I was sitting there next to my father while there was like, you know, the stripper and that whole kind of thing, I was probably thinking, *Whoa, this is weird*. But it was fine.

There was a whole big climax. Everybody was egging my dad on. So he lay down on some chairs. And the stripper literally was grinding it down on his face. And everybody was like, "Hey Jack, you've got to get up there, too." And there's this chick and my father—and I was like, "No way . . . it's enough." Still, I think everyone was kind of psyched that I was there. I don't think it fazed anyone.

The funny thing is, I was also the best man at a friend's wedding a few years ago and we did his bachelor party out in Las Vegas. It was ridiculous. We went to the glitziest strip club, got a table, and dropped insane amounts of money. It was very important to the groom that he have this really great send-off into married life. He just wanted it to be well planned and a big deal—you know, really do "the Vegas thing," so we really played on that. I decided to make the whole theme of it be that we hadn't planned anything and that we were just getting surprised by stuff. Like, "Let's go talk to that limo driver and just see if we can hop in the back" . . . of the car we had *ordered*. It was just to piss him off, because he kind of deserved it.

My dad's was just so different from my friends' bachelor parties, because there was no pressure. When it's your second marriage, there's not the same feel to it at all. It was just an excuse to have a party.

Infamous Bachelor Parties:
THOMAS BRUDERMAN, 2003

The bachelor bacchanal for this Fidelity Investments' trader incorporated a dwarf, a private jet and yacht, two prostitutes, several suites at South Beach's Delano Hotel, and cost in excess of $100,000. Two years after Bruderman's last hurrah, the SEC launched an investigation of the party. Their beef: It appears that corporate bigwigs who do business with Fidelity, including father of the bride/defamed Tyco chief **Dennis Kozlowski**, paid for all or part of the extravagant bash. According to the *Daily News*, the father of the groom explained, "It wasn't like a three-ring circus. It was a nice party. There was only one dwarf."

THE INNOCENT BYSTANDER
Spike D.

Like an animal sensing a trap about to snap shut, even the calmest, most contented of men can be unnerved by an impending wedding. The bachelor party only makes matters worse by drawing attention to what they are hypothetically "giving up." It's only natural that they would vent their last-minute jitters and fleeting second thoughts during their final fling. But what if all of your friends think you shouldn't go through with it? And what if they wait to mention it until twelve hours before the wedding, at the bachelor party? Spike D. was privy to that kind of "clusterfuck" ten years ago in Seattle.

It was one of those classic setups: I didn't know the person getting married very well; I was a good friend of a number of the groomsmen, and they were all friends from high school.

But I would always hear these stories about the groom's relationship with his then-girlfriend. She was ten years older, and it was widely suspected that they were getting married because she had intentionally gotten herself pregnant. Everyone was very concerned. They sort of felt like it was an entrapment thing.

Then I met her, and I started to understand why they suspected it. She was an incredibly needy person, one of those people where it's kind of painful standing near them, because you can *feel* their neediness—their need for approval and attention. It's overwhelming.

The groom was twenty-three at the time and she was

thirty-three—so she was really excited to be pregnant. We were all pretty ambivalent about it, including the groom-to-be. I remember asking him, "So, you're gettin' married?" And there was this storm cloud on his face and he was like, "That's what they tell me." It was this terribly passive construction, like, "Well, that's what's happening to me." Like cancer. I wanted to be like, "Dude, you *choose* your wife. You don't *have* to get married."

The groom got very, very angry, because people don't like interventions—especially at their bachelor party.

So that's sort of the prelude to the bachelor party, which was the night before the wedding. We went to these cheesy strip clubs in Seattle, which all have a lot of rules about public touching. And they have rules about distance, and there's certainly no alcohol. So people are drinking Diet Coke, and everyone's unhappy already. Although, someone had brought a bottle of Jägermeister and everyone was doing shots of it illicitly at the clubs or between places. And everyone's getting pretty fucked up.

It was really lining up to be a standard but boring event. Then, right near the end of the evening, the groom was complaining about the wedding ceremony—specifically that he only has one part in the whole ceremony, where he has to give a reading. And so my friend asks him, "Well, what are you reading?" And he's like, "Well, they're making me read it." And he then confesses that it's an Emily Dickinson poem—an Emily Dickinson poem that's been *chosen* for him.

That is the moment when everything turned. My friend was like, "We need to talk." Then he starts the intervention right there. He doesn't coordinate with the other people, although we all sort of thought, *Maybe somebody should talk to him.* We had been talking about that forever, but no one had ever said, "Maybe we should do it the *night before* at the strip club." Once we got to the club, everyone assumed there were no more exit strategies.

So when our friend said, "We need to talk," and sort of sidled up to him, everybody else knew. We were like, *Oh my God, he's pulling the trigger.* And so he starts telling the groom, "You don't have to do this. You could leave right now, and we could just drive away." And we're all nodding, like, "We actually can just drive away."

At first, the groom was just sullen, listening, and I thought, *Is this actually gonna work? We could be so* Thelma and Louise. It was sort of exciting. Maybe this is the ultimate personification of doing the groomsman's job. Like maybe the top job is, if the person is not actually supposed to get married, then the people he's asked to back him up at the wedding should be able to tell him that.

But at some point the groom—who was *really* drunk—was

like, "No! No! What are you talkin' about?" And then it turned ugly, and people were exchanging words, and then people had to intercede to make sure it didn't come to blows. And the groom got very, very angry, because people don't like interventions—especially at their bachelor party. And he's like, "How dare you! You ruined my wedding!"

We're still at the strip club. There are women gyrating, and periodically they would come up to us, and they would see people arguing and then kind of slink away. That was pretty much the end of whatever good mood there was—I mean, there wasn't a good mood to begin with. And the only solution was to drink—heavily.

I think we kept drinking because no one knew what to say, and no one wanted the evening to end with everyone so angry and talking about their feelings. So it was a very effective strategy. All hail the evolved male of the species! And I'm a great communicator, but it was just not a case where communicating was gonna help, because the more clearly people communicate, the clearer it would become that tomorrow's a fucked proposition. *Get out! Get out!*

I was so fucked up when they picked me up the next day to go to the wedding. My friend, who started the intervention, was driving. I was sitting in the front seat looking at the road, and I say, "I, uh . . . I think I'm still drunk." And I look over at my friend and I know that he must be drunk too.

There was a lot of talk in the car about the groom. How upset was he? How much will he remember? But then we saw him when we arrived. He was in his tux and he looked emotionally vacant, which was probably the worst thing. We couldn't tell if he was upset or not. When he greeted us, he was like, "Hey, here we are. This is it." And the conversation was all about the day's events, not about last night or the future.

The capper was when he read the Emily Dickinson poem, which was dreadful. "A spider . . . walked . . ." I don't know what it was; I can't remember, probably because I was very busy trying not to laugh or cry.

We didn't stay very long at the reception, not as long as we probably should have. And I think we were in better shape leaving the reception than when we arrived, which is pretty rare for a wedding.

Spike only saw the groom once or twice after that. And nobody ever talked about the bachelor party, until Spike mentioned it a few months ago. "They tried to make it *un*-happen. In fact, when I brought it up, everyone acted as though I had actually given them permission to talk about it." In case you're wondering, the couple had the baby and stayed together for eight years. Both are currently single.

Urban Legends
& Bachelor Parties

Bachelor and bachelorette parties are popular settings for many urban myths. And most of them deliver the same moral: Cheaters beware.

THE NAUGHTY GROOM

The groom sleeps with the maid of honor at his bachelor party, and the bride gets her hands on a photo. She duplicates the photo, tapes one to the bottom of each guest's chair, and then asks that everyone look under their chair during the reception. In another version, the groom takes revenge on *her* cheating by making her parents pay for a three-hundred-person wedding before revealing the duplicity—and his plan to leave her—during his wedding speech.

THE BAD BACHELORETTE

A white woman married to a white man gives birth to a black baby nine months after her wild bachelorette party, which featured a male stripper who, you guessed it, was black. In other versions of this legend, it's the husband who sleeps with a black female stripper. And it's twins that are born: one white and one black.

DEATH BY CLEAVAGE

GROOM SUFFOCATED BY STRIPPER'S MASSIVE BREASTS AT BACHELOR PARTY! Sounds like a tabloid headline? Well, it was first "reported" in that bastion of untruths, *Weekly World News*. The Internet—specifically Yahoo!'s "Latest News & Gossip" page—helped it spread from there.

LOUSY LUCK

An aggressive bride-to-be gets onstage at a male strip club. One of the dancers flings his G-string at her and it lands on her face. She wakes up the next morning with an inflamed eye. Turns out he had pubic lice, one of which took up residence in the bride's face (or, in a more believable variant, she winds up with lice in her eyebrows).

CONDOM CLUELESS

Like most grooms, the one in this tale swears he won't do anything untoward with the strippers at his bachelor party. But according to popular mythology, he sleeps with a talented stripper who, unbeknownst to him, rolls a condom onto his penis. When he returns home from the party, his fiancée is awake. And as he undresses, a rubber filled with evidence falls out of his pants. Busted!

THE SOBER BACHELOR
Angelo T.

Angelo T. had no doubts about getting married, but his bachelor party in 2005 was still a test. See, Angelo doesn't drink; it's a survival strategy for the former heroin addict. "I was a fuck-up; I started drinking on a regular basis when I was like fourteen and started smoking pot shortly thereafter," he explains. "When I moved to New York City for college, it really just took off. Within a month I had a heroin habit that I kept for the next three years. I ended up dropping out of college, and went from being an Ivy League student to an inmate at Rikers Island in not that long of a time. So it was hard for me to argue that I could drink or use drugs successfully." Most of his friends still drink and, per his instructions, they did not hold back during his prewedding bash at a friend's SoHo loft.

I'm not someone who's like, "If I can't drink, then no one should." If you can smoke pot and drink on a regular basis and still have meaningful relationships and hold down a job, then fuck it. In fact I told my friends that I wanted someone to throw up at my bachelor party, because that just seemed like the right thing to do. You know, if we're going to have a bachelor party, let's go ahead and *do* it.

It was actually a low-key evening until midnight. People were drinking and we were playing cards. Then the strippers showed up and everything pretty much went crazy. We're watching two girls screw each other with strap-ons. And it was really over the top and what someone would think a bachelor party should be in terms of male hormonal chaos.

At that point I could tell just how much people had drank. And people are willing to do things when they're drunk that they wouldn't otherwise find as appealing. Normally people don't pour beer on each other, and they don't scream and yell and jump up and down and kick stuff. And the strippers certainly didn't have any inhibitions about what they were doing; I guess that signaled to everybody else that they shouldn't either.

I once heard someone say, "If you keep going to a barbershop, eventually you're gonna get your hair cut," which is kind of like a drug addict going to a big party.

I wasn't tempted to drink at the party. When I know I'm going to go into a situation like that, I mentally prepare myself for what I'm going to see. It's kind of hard to explain—I just reaffirm what I'm doing. In other words, "I'm staying clean. And I'm just going out to hang out with friends." But part of staying clean is staying

even though I was clean, it didn't mean that I couldn't have a
bachelor party.

I've come pretty far in the past ten years. The wedding was
kind of a culmination, a chance to take stock of my life, which
has actually turned out pretty well: I go to law school, I married
someone who's responsible and cute, I have a job lined up for
when I graduate, I pay my rent, and I'm certainly happy when I
wake up in the morning. Knowing that my life hasn't always been
this way, and knowing that it could have been very different, makes
it *all* more meaningful.

THE REMORSEFUL BEST MAN
Brent P.

**Even for the sober, alcohol is a big part of the ritual, so maybe it
shouldn't be shocking that injuries and deaths occur at bachelor**

parties. In the past year alone, I have read stories about fatal car crashes, savage beatings, and a murder. In one case, the jealous groom and his buddies allegedly stopped their bachelor party fun when they learned the ladies were enjoying a male dancer across town. They showed up at the bride's bachelorette party and someone stabbed the dancer. No doubt, many more incidents go unreported and undiscussed.

Brent P. tries not to dwell on what happened at his buddy's bachelor party more than two decades ago, but he decided to talk with me, in part because he hopes his story will serve as a warning to others.

One of my best friends from high school, Jim, was getting married to a girl named Tracey, who he had met at the seafood restaurant that we all worked at in Phoenix. We were a tight crew; the employees basically ran the restaurant and we did whatever we wanted to. And we were all in our early to mid twenties.

I decided to throw Jim's bachelor party, and we were going to go to Las Vegas, so I got a bus and invited almost a dozen people. We were going to leave in the morning to have a night in Vegas to party and come back the next day. On the way, we planned to stop at a lake.

So we were on the bus and, you know, we had beers in coolers. One of the employees who worked with us was a younger busboy named Tommy. I was unaware that he'd gotten into the coolers and started drinking.

So we get to this lake and they have a water park with slides and ropes and things you can jump off of. And we all signed a waiver of liability.

It's a hot day and the cicadas are going. We start swimming around and Tommy jumps in headfirst. Somebody had seen him jump in, but it didn't occur to anybody that he didn't come up. A few minutes go by and the groom's brother says, "Where's Tommy?"

We can't find him and we start thinking maybe he's underwater. And the water is black, so we couldn't see anything, and I think there was only one lifeguard to look after all these people. So people started diving down, feeling the murky bottom. And it took a few minutes and finally someone who wasn't with our group pulled him up by the wrist and said, "I got him."

One guy with us was a nurse and the groom's brother was a chiropractor. And these two guys started doing CPR on the shore. And it's really hot, and people are just standing around stunned and silent. This goes on for a few minutes. And they called the paramedics, who took maybe twenty minutes to get there, because we're in the middle of the desert.

In the meantime, I'm distraught and I actually called my dad, who's a lawyer, because I was worried about *my* liability since I organized the party. He said not to worry, and I was crying. I mean, I was upset.

The paramedics came and somebody said they got a heartbeat, and everybody cheered. They took Tommy to the nearest hospital, which is miles and miles down the road, and we followed in the bus. We waited around the hospital for a couple of hours, and they finally came out and told us that he was dead.

Two of the schmucks that were on the bus said, "What do we

do? Keep going to Vegas? Tommy would have wanted us to." Like the deceased would have wanted us to party, right? And I looked at these guys, and I said, "You're out of your minds. We're not going to Vegas. Somebody just *died*. We've got to go home and somebody's got to tell his parents."

So we got on the bus and we went back to Phoenix. Eventually Tommy's parents were told and he was buried. But nothing ever happened—they didn't sue the lake or anything like that.

We thought Tommy was an idiot for getting too drunk, but it could've happened to anybody. It's something I probably wouldn't have done, because I've been a diver for a long time, and you watch your head and neck when you're jumping around in shallow water. But he didn't have that experience.

It was bad. It crosses my mind every once in a while, but it didn't get to me or haunt me or anything like that. It's just a sad episode. It shouldn't have happened.

THE BRIDE'S IMPOSTOR
Richard D.

As you might imagine, sometimes the entertainment gets caught in the drama. Celebrity impersonator Richard D. thought he had the gig of a lifetime performing at David Gest's bachelor party as bride-to-be Liza Minnelli. The only problem: It was a surprise for Gest who was none too thrilled when he found out.

I must have been nine years old the first time I saw Liza. *Cabaret* was on TV. And I remember turning to my mother and saying, "I want to meet that lady." I don't think she was impressed, but I was. Liza was this free spirit, and to a child, that was infectious. And of course her character was in this nightclub and entertaining, and I thought that was all kinds of cool.

By the time David and Liza were getting married, I had been impersonating Liza for three or four years. And I did a lot of private clubs and parties—that's where you make your bread and butter.

At first I was called about the wedding shower they were planning for Liza at Denise Rich's home on Park Avenue. It was going to be a Kit Kat Club, *Cabaret* thing: All the waiters were going to be dressed up and they wanted a Liza impersonator to do "Cabaret." Of course I said yes—what a great honor! But it was kind of nerve-racking, you know, to perform in front of her in a room without the proper sound equipment and just a little boom box.

Supposedly David said, "I don't think Liza would be into this. I think this is one step too far." The long and short of it is, David got her a gig for the night her wedding shower was supposed to happen, probably for a lot of money, and they changed her shower to a Wednesday afternoon and made it much shorter. So they didn't need me, which was fine. I'd prefer she come to see my show, with the sound and the lights and the costumes.

About a week later, an agent called me. He was a friend of David's and he said they were going to have a bachelor party for him. "We need an impersonator to perform live. Would you be interested? Just know there are going to be a lot of celebrities there—so keep cool." And there were: Michael and Tito Jackson were there, and Ben Vereen. And I'm like, "That doesn't faze me at all." The only person that sort of gets me juicy is Liza. Other than that, it's just people in the business.

I arrived early at the party, and when I got out of my cab, somebody yelled, "Liza!" I turned and there were photographers from the London press, and the *Post* and the *Daily News*. Honestly, I was taken a little off guard.

Having three drag queens at your bachelor party is kind of an odd thing, especially if they're dressed as your wife.

When they knew that David was coming in, his friends wanted all of the Liza impersonators at the front door—there were three of us, but I was the only one that was performing; the other two were just walking around being Liza at a party. David started walking through, and when he saw us, he turned and sort of backed up a little and said something like, "Oh, no," or "Oh, shit"; he was not pleased.

Then the *Post* said they wanted a picture of me and David together, like with me on his lap. And he was like, "No way!" He wasn't having it, and I don't think I would have done it anyway. Publicity is great, and some people believe any publicity is good, but I don't need that kind of publicity. And neither did he. I mean, having three drag queens at your bachelor party is kind of an odd thing, especially if they're dressed as your wife. And I think he knew what they were after: They wanted to suggest he was gay, because I think people were already thinking, [*singing*] "You're a queer one, Julie Jordan."[2]

If it wasn't for us, it would have been a fucking boring party. And when it was all said and done, it was in a lot of papers.

It was a little uncomfortable at first, but the show went on. I kept it short, and at one point David gave me the thumbs-up. Obviously he realized I was not there to make fun of his wife-to-be.

I really felt like Cinderella that night. I don't mean to be egotistical about it, but the evening was slightly about me being there . . . you know, about three impersonators being there. To be honest, if it wasn't for us, it would have been a fucking boring party. And when it was all said and done, it was in the *Post*, it was in the *Globe*—it was in a lot of papers. And there was my picture.

When I saw it in the *Post*, I almost started bawling. I mean, hey, I'm an actor. I enjoy a little bit of attention—even in a dress.

2 **"You're a Queer One, Julie Jordon"** (n) Title of a song from the musical *Carousel*, about a tumultuous love affair between a traveling carnie and a local factory worker

THE CLOSETED CHRISTIAN
Todd M.

Todd M., a former Christian pop singer, is no stranger to tricky situations. As a teen, he struggled with his sexuality as he was performing for crowds of the faithful. Now thirty-five, Todd recounts a bachelor party he attended when he was nineteen. It was for the brother of his best friend, Barry.

I remember a lot of khakis: *every* person had on a pair of khakis and a golf shirt. I, of course, was wearing something very festive, but simple—a Versace shirt that was white but had a faint blue and black pattern on it—and it was a *little* bit see-through. And I was wearing white Theory trousers—which is Hugo Boss's ready-to-wear line—with black Ferragamo wedge sandals.

I was out to Barry and his brother George, but not to any of his friends. But they all knew that I was gay. In fact George's friend Ron called me "gerbil-jammer."

Ron was the best man and the organizer of the bachelor party. It was held in a hotel room that had a living room, a little kitchenette, a separate bedroom, a couple of bathrooms, and a hot tub outside. There were bottles of liquor everywhere and a cooler of beer, and the refrigerator was full of Jell-O shots that someone had made. It was the equivalent of a housewives' Tupperware potluck party, where everybody brought a dish; in this case, everybody brought a bottle of booze and a bag of dope.

So everyone was sitting around and all of a sudden a very large African-American man came to the door. Based on every movie that I had seen in my sheltered suburban life, he was everything like a pimp. Next were the girls: these three beaten-up-by-life, shuffling-through-on-clay-feet gals. These were not "good girls," as my mother would have said.

One thing we did have in common was that, deep down, neither of us really wanted to be there.

There were two brunettes and a blonde. The blonde was a combination of something out of *The Best Little Whorehouse in Texas* and *Oliver Twist*. And one brunette had sort of black hair that she had dyed at home in her sink. She was a cross between Dolly Parton and Elvira: She had big, big, big tits, but she looked like a vampire.

When I saw these three girls come in, I remember feeling an enormous sense of responsibility, like these girls really need help, and maybe I can be their Oprah. And I'd had a couple of drinks and God knows how many bong hits.

While two of the girls were working the room, the other was sitting in the bedroom, and I went in and actually said to her, "Why do you do this? Does he beat you?" I had already assumed that they were being held captive. And she said, "'Cause I make good *muh-ney*; I *like* what I do!" Which was a very surprising answer to me.

I realized at that point that my work there was done; this girl was seemingly happy in what she was doing. And even if she wasn't, she sure as hell was not going to come out to a *fag* at a bachelor party in Ohio. Honestly, what the hell do we have in common? I think the one thing we did have in common was that deep down, neither of us really *wanted* to be there.

As the evening progressed, these men in their khakis and their golf shirts reverted to some sort of sophomoric behavior. They had no conscience about anything, about women, about their wives. The best man, Ron, was married—I knew his wife and his kids—and he was the ringleader of this whole thing. I don't think you can say this about all men in the suburbs, but I think some men of certain character are, um, willing to go there. And they take the opportunity when it comes.

The girls put on some music and they began to strip and dance—all the things I imagine you would see at a seedy titty bar. And the guys were putting dollar bills in their bras and their panties. And I thought, *God, if you can make that much in your bras and panties, why take them off?*

But then of course the clothing came off, and they found more creative ways to retrieve their fare. A man would take a dollar bill or a five-dollar bill, fold it lengthwise, then lie down on the floor and put the bill on his nose. And a girl would straddle the guy's face and bend down in this very seductive, sexual way and—*pop!*—pick up the bill with her . . . well, my mother always called it a "bunny." You know, boys had birds and girls had bunnies.

Of course Ron was really trying to get me involved. He said, "C'mon, Todd. Here's the money, here's a five." And he sort of began to tug at my arm, because I was in the kitchenette huddled in the corner in the fetal position, probably reciting the words of a Madonna song slowly and calmly in my mind, trying to find my gayness. But he was really pulling me out into the middle of the room. And now the attention was on me. People were looking: *Is this guy gonna do it?*

It was like one of those moments in a movie, when the music stops and everybody on the high school dance floor stops dancing and turns around. And I said, "Goddammit, Ron, no! First of all, do you know how dirty money is? Do you know how many times a day that bill changes hands? It's filthy! I'm not putting that anywhere near, on, or about my face. Secondly, look at this girl: She is a breeding ground for bacteria. God knows where she has been. I'm sorry, I'm not able to participate." And I went back to the kitchenette, victorious. And they sort of blew it off. They were all drunk and whatever, and they said, "Faggot," and this and that and the other thing.

After the party was officially over, Ron and one of the other groomsmen took the gals down to the hot tub. You could see through the bushes from the parking lot. And as we were leaving, I saw Ron and this other guy making out with two of these girls. I'm assuming these girls weren't overcome with their looks and never said, "Oh, I met the man of my dreams at this gig." I think they were paid to have sex with these two married groomsmen. And for me, that was the cherry on the cake of dirty.

The next day, I sang at the wedding. It was in this big,

gorgeous Catholic church. I sang the Lord's Prayer a cappella. And I remember all the groomsmen had on purple boutonnieres and black tuxedoes. They all looked so clean and tidy. And their wives were wearing floral prints. And their children were wearing the opaque stockings with the patent-leather shoes. And everybody was all cleaned up.

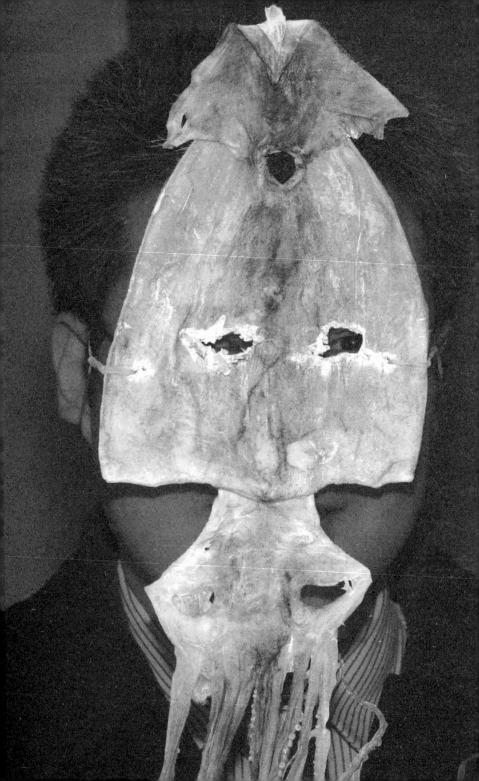

Chapter 7

It's a Small World After All

A WEDDING IS ONE OF THE MOST SIGNIFICANT, sacred occasions in practically every culture on the planet, so it's not surprising that there is a wide range of rituals leading up to the big day. Some of these rituals may seem bizarre to an outsider. In China, for instance, part of the run up to marriage includes the installation of the bridal bed the day before the wedding. The groom oversees his friends' handiwork, and once the bed is in place, as many kids as possible climb into the bed to encourage the bride's fertility. On the Scottish Isle of Orkney, there's the customary "fit-washing," or foot washing, the night before the wedding.

Even though they go by different names—"stag do" in Great Britain, "bucks party" in Australia, *"junggesellenabschied"* in Germany, *"svensexa"* in Sweden, and "bachelor party" in the

United States—men-only rituals are part of the prewedding itinerary in most Western countries. All of the bashes have a few things in common: There's plenty of liquor involved, there's typically some sexual rumblings, and the party implies the end of an era for the groom and his friends. Of course each country and community puts its own twist on the ritual.

THE AUSTRALIAN PRANKSTER
Liam K.

The centerpiece of the Australian bucks party is a sometimes elaborate, somewhat sadistic prank. Thirty-one-year-old Liam K., who admits, "I look forward to the bucks more than the wedding," told me about one such prank that quickly became a staple of my cocktail-party repertoire.

The most memorable one was for a guy I play rugby with. We all met at ten a.m. and started by smoking dope. We had already decided to play "pub golf" around Sydney. I suspect you don't know what that is, mate. There's eighteen pubs, and each pub has a different par to it, like a par three or a par four. You go into each pub for twenty minutes or so. And if it's a par three, you have to drink three beers while you're there. But if you get four beers in you, then you go one-under par. And it's a competition to see who can have the lowest score.

By the end of the eighteen holes—I mean pubs—it's pretty severe. For this bucks, we had a bus taking us from one pub to the other. By about seven p.m., the groom was unconscious. The normal thing would have been to strip him and leave him somewhere. But the best man said, "Why don't we take him to the hospital, put a cast on his arm, and pretend he's broken it. By the time we got to the hospital, it turned into, "Fuck it, we're gonna put a cast on his whole leg," from his ankle to the top of his hip. And because one of the guys we play rugby with is a doctor at the hospital, they let us do it.

The groom woke up the next day, and we told him he fell down the stairs at a pub and broke his leg. He didn't know it wasn't broken, because his leg was in the cast and he couldn't move it.

The wedding was two or three days later, so he went through the wedding on crutches with a cast. For his honeymoon, he went to Fiji. He was there for ten days and didn't swim because he figured he couldn't get his cast wet.

We told him when he got back. He didn't talk to us for a long time. We're still on bad terms with his missus—and that was five fuckin' years ago. He laughs about it now, but he can still get pissed if we all laugh about it too much.

Another memorable one was in a Chinese restaurant and we had a private room. We had one stripper come in and drop hot wax all over the groom and she burned his chest hair. And she got him to lay on the ground with a dildo in his mouth and she sort of squatted up and down on it. This was in front of the bride's father! Straight after she left, we had a fatty-gram[1] come in and sort of rub

....

[1] fatty-gram (n) an obese female stripper; similar to "fat mamas" in the United States

her tits on him with whipped cream. And he actually ended up picking up a broad that night after his father-in-law went home.

I don't know if there's any massive differences between the Australian and American parties. In Australia, it tends to be a night, or a day and a night, whereas the American ones tend to be more, "Let's get out of town and hit Vegas or Cabo."

The one American bachelor party I went to was for a week in Cabo San Lucas, Mexico. That was probably the sleaziest one I've ever been on, because the groom banged a few birds.[2] And actually they wouldn't let him back in the country because he lost his voice and he had bruises all over him—and he doesn't really look that much like his passport. So it took us a few hours to get through your Immigration, which was actually pretty funny.

GOING GLOBAL BULGARIA

On the morning of the wedding, friends pour barley over the Bulgarian groom and fire rifles into the air to ward off evil spirits. Next up, a lively processional to the best man's house, where the groom presents him with wine and a baked chicken. From that point on, the best man's word is law as far as the wedding goes. The best woman (often the best man's wife) and the best man then lead the procession to the bride's house, where they present the bride with wine, a bridal veil, candles, and baked sweets.

2 **birds** (n) slang, young women

THE FINNISH FRIEND
Niko L.

Bachelor parties in Finland are called *polttarit*. "I have no idea where that word comes from," notes Niko L., who lives in Helsinki, "but the word it's closest to is *polttaa*, which translates to 'to burn.' Maybe the wise, ancient Finns tried to burn the bachelor to stop him from getting married." Much like the Australian incarnation, the Finn's version includes a prank and some soft-core humiliation.

Part of the ritual is that you dress the bachelor in a funny costume and have him walk around the city. He may, for example, have to sell something that nobody wants for some cheap sum. Like, "Pay one euro to kiss me." Some people don't really like the tradition, because sometimes it goes too far. I don't know if it's much fun for the person getting married, but it's great fun for people who want to punish their friend.

Most of the bachelor parties I've been to, we went to a nice restaurant and maybe went bowling or did something not that special—just something we wouldn't do on a normal weekend. But with this one bachelor, everyone wanted to test the limits, because he's the kind of guy who always has to have the best story. He boasts about hanging out with the Hell's Angels or standing up to some guy at work. Basically he talks about situations that he gets into and how he's the hero who saves the day. Naturally, because he has a big mouth, we wanted to really scare him.

His *polttarit* was in Helsinki. The first thing he needed to do was collect money for a costume from people passing by. And then he had to buy the costume. We went to an open-air flea market and he found a pink ballet costume; it was five euros or something small.

He put on the costume and we made him swim in the sea a little bit. It's something that many bachelor parties do. They drop the guy in the harbor in an inner tube and everyone on the shore throws something at him. We just made him do a quick dip, and it was in the summer, so it wasn't cold. In fact it was so sunny he got burned really bad in that costume.

Then we walked around the city for a little while and went to eat. There were maybe twenty people in our party, and we went to a Greek restaurant. Everybody got to order whatever they wanted and so did the groom, but we had instructed the restaurant to bring him some kind of porridge, regardless of what he ordered. So everybody else was eating really well, but he had to eat porridge for the whole dinner.

He was quite unmoved the whole day, saying things like, "This is nothing! Is this the best you can come up with?" But after we ate, we blindfolded him. Then we walked one or two kilometers so he really didn't have any clue where he was, and we took him to a kinky party.[3] I haven't been to very many kinky parties, but you can imagine what it would be: lots of people with plastic or PVC costumes; people had other people on leashes or whatever.

Nothing extreme yet, but then we tied him to a cross—a frame that basically had him standing in an X position with his feet

....

3 **kinky party** (n) a fetish party with an emphasis on the erotic and exotic

and hands fastened. The DJ at the party, who was also a friend, started to play more and more aggressive music while the regular partygoers gathered around the cross. The bachelor was still blind-folded, smiling in anticipation of what was to come. Then comes this guy with a blowtorch and an iron marker, the kind that's used for branding animals. He starts to heat the marker. The music intensifies, the crowd gets ready for the first live show of their kinky evening: human branding! The hot iron is glowing red. And *then* we took off the blindfold. You should have seen the poor bastard's face. He nearly peed his pants—or ballet costume, actually.

We didn't really brand him, but afterward he called his wife-to-be and told her that he was branded with this mark. She was screaming and really thinking we had really gone too far with it.

GOING GLOBAL
GERMANY

Dating back at least to the Middle Ages, the German *polterabend* (translation: "rumble/beat evening") occurred the night before the wedding. Back then, the idea was to make as much noise as possible to scare away those darn evil spirits. Men and women, family and friends gathered at the couple's future residence and threw pots and broke plates. The next morning, the couple collected what shattered and somehow it was good luck. Now the ritual seems to be more like a co-ed version of the exclusively male German ritual, *junggesellenabschied* (translation: "bachelor parting"), and resembles the American bachelor party.

THE EGYPTIAN SPY
Youssef M.

Even though Egypt is one of the more liberal and Westernized countries in the Middle East, there's no ritualized naughty for grooms in this predominantly Muslim culture. "Sometimes if a man is getting married, his friends will make a party for him, but it's not a tradition and there's no name for it," explains Youssef M., a thirty-one-year-old academic from Cairo. But for women there is the henna[4] party, which dates back to ancient Egypt. "The henna is a big celebration," he adds. "Sometimes it's as big as the wedding."

All of the women get together, usually the night before the wedding: relatives, friends of the bride, females from the family of the groom. They celebrate, they eat, they dance, and they make drawings with the henna, usually on the hands or the feet of the bride. Those drawings last for a week or two, so you can see them the next day at the wedding. Men are not allowed, except for the groom.

This celebration was normally for villagers or lower classes. But now it is also a tradition for the upper and middle classes. It's interesting, because usually for lower classes, it's a very simple celebration: There's a couple of drums and dancing, and someone makes a henna paste.

Now, because a lot of the upper classes are also starting to do

....

4 henna (n) reddish-brown dye made from leaves of henna plants; often used ritualistically to creat elaborate designs symbolizing fertility and prosperity

this kind of celebration, it's gotten very fancy. They hire a DJ to play Egyptian pop, and they have catering, and they hire a professional woman whose job it is just to make drawings. She'll be sitting there with the henna and she may even have a book, so you can choose the design and say, "I want this one and that size."

I have actually attended a henna party, because my sister was getting married and it was done at our house. So I just happened to be there and I was watching. There was a lot, a lot of food. The women were wearing what they would normally wear to a party, and some wore the galabeeyah, which is the traditional Egyptian dress.

I was surprised: all of these women, who were normally very serious and didn't usually dance in the presence of men, suddenly they were very outgoing and everybody's dancing. I wasn't just watching all night. At some point I was mingling and eating and talking to my aunts.

The women really didn't care that I was there. Of course, if my family was extremely religious, they would have separated the men and women anyway. But our family is not that conservative. Also, I was quite young—maybe eighteen—so to them, I wasn't like a grown man.

Why do you think there's a celebration for brides, but not grooms?

Traditionally, Egyptian men have had more freedom than women, and men could just go off and party anyway. But for women, the henna was an opportunity to get together and dance, which was probably not something that happened very often for a young Egyptian woman—

I'm talking in the old days, not nowadays. I think also, in the old days, this was a night when other girls would give a bath to the bride and remove the hair from private parts. And I'm sure there were tips about sex stuff from the girls who already got married. I think women are still very proud of the henna and they like that it's their own thing. A man can attend every now and then, but I don't think they would like if it were a combined event. And a lot of women are still much more comfortable when they are alone with other women.

THE IRAQI EXPERIENCE
Zeyad A.

Hennas are also big in Iraq according to Zeyad A., a blogger from Baghdad. "Most henna occasions in Iraq are segregated these days; there is a separate occasion for male friends of the groom, and another for the bride and female relatives. People differentiate and say 'the men's henna' and 'the women's henna,'" he explains. Zeyad attended a men's henna recently for a friend of his from high school, even as a war raged all around.

Even though there's fighting going on, the henna rituals still take place, since they are a very significant part of weddings, especially for women. But people are now wary of staying out late, so the occasion usually takes place much earlier than it used to, and sometimes relatives who live in other parts of town have to spend the night.

My friend's henna was at his house two days before the wedding. It started around five p.m. and ended at eight p.m., whereas in the past they would start at seven p.m. or later and end at midnight. It was attended by close friends of the groom, his male relatives, and neighbors. We sat in the garden and a DJ was playing some traditional and popular Iraqi music for about two hours or so, and then we had dinner: *quzi*[5] with kebabs and salads.

We were standing around the dinner table outside in the garden and everyone was eating and chatting. Then we heard an ear-shattering blast. We counted five ambulances racing away and sirens wailing. Most people just looked up from their plates, joked about the incident, and then went on eating. Another friend took out a video camera and started filming while gunshots were raging close by. A few people who lived nearby were concerned and called their relatives or neighbors to inquire about the blast, and many people finished their food quickly so that they could return home before there were any unexpected developments.

I left with another friend who lived near the explosion site, the Ali Bash *husseiniya*.[6] We didn't directly go to see what happened—that would be a foolish thing to do—but we finished our food and thanked our host. We stopped about twenty minutes after the explosion, which was most likely caused by a BMW rigged with explosives. Iraqi National Guard and soldiers had already blocked the streets, and they were warning people not to go in that direction because there were rumors of a second rigged vehicle. There was sporadic gunfire—soldiers usually shoot in the air to prevent curious people from coming close to the explosion area. We asked some people what was going on and listened to their versions of the story, and then we drove away, taking side streets instead of the main road.

....

5 quzi (n) a traditional Iraqi dish of roasted lamb
6 husseiniya (n) a Muslim community center, typically used for study and prayer

THE KOREAN TRADITION
Jin K.

For Koreans and Korean Americans, the wedding is preceded not by a simply hedonistic party, but by a more elaborate "ham," or gift box delivery ceremony. "The gift box tradition is that the friends of the groom come to the bride's house the night before the wedding and they bring boxes of gifts," explains Korean-American Jin K. "They're dressed up in traditional clothing—fun stuff—and their faces are supposed to be painted black with squid's ink. I don't know why. I asked my mom and she doesn't know why either."

According to historian Laurel Kendall, author of *Getting Married in Korea*, "When the groom's friends bring the gift box containing the marriage contract and betrothal gifts, they bargain and banter with the bride's family in the hope of extorting from them a large 'delivery fee.' The money they receive is usually spent on an evening's expansive and expensive celebration."[7] Koreans in Jin's California community do it a little differently.

The friends of the groom come in as though they're selling the boxes, saying, "Box for sale!" in Korean. The bride's family and the bride herself go and greet the groom's party with money and food as if they're accepting the sale. It's really just an excuse for a party, it seems to me.

....

7 Kendall, Laurel. *Getting Married in Korea*. Berkeley: University of California Press, 1996.

I've never been to a wedding where they do it the traditional way, not in Korea and not in the States. We didn't do the black face or costumes—people just dress up really nice and bring lots of gifts to the bride and her family and friends.

It's really just an excuse for a party.

For my cousin's wedding, her fiancé's friends—some guys, but mostly girls, all in their thirties or younger—came over to her house with little boxes of stuff: anything from Tiffany jewelry to gift certificates to fancy restaurants to prank gifts, like sex toys. But a lot of the stuff they brought her was really, really expensive.

In return, her mom had set up this big, fancy catered dinner in their house for the groom's friends. It was really just like this big party for all the young people, since the wedding itself was really expensive and for the adults only. It wasn't the traditional way, but I've been to a million weddings recently and every gift box night seems a little bit different—and more and more expensive each year.

Five Questions for Tim Relf, author of the acclaimed novel *Stag*

British author Tim Relf's surprisingly emotional book *Stag* focuses on a thirty-year-old who gets together with his close friends for a stag party in their old college town. Turns out, everyone else has gotten hitched, learned about moderation, and moved on. But Relf's main character is newly single, addicted to booze, and a total mess.

What inspired you to write *Stag*?

Stag parties range from the hilarious to the horrifying—and can be everything in between. Perfect fiction material, in other words. It wasn't any one stag in particular that prompted me to write the book, but I went to more than twenty between the ages of eighteen and thirty, and they left a massive impression on me. I always knew I'd write about them one day. Plus I wanted to write a book that featured alcohol, because then all the time I'd spent in bars would count as research!

Why set it at a stag party, as opposed to a reunion or a wedding?

Other social events tend to involve mixed groups, but the stag party is one of the few gatherings nowadays that is exclusively male. This brings out the best and the worst in men! We can be bawdy, aggressive, and arrogant, but we're also loyal, sensitive, and vulnerable. They involve people getting together and drinking heavily with old friends a long way away from their hometown, so emotions get amplified. It's inevitably a recipe for comedy and tragedy. The main character in my book is a normal, everyday guy who's just beginning to realize he likes the booze a little too much. So, from a fictional point of view, where better to set the story than at the one event where any notions of restraint disappear?

Describe the perfect stag party.

That depends on how old you are. When I was in my twenties, it would have involved huge quantities of alcohol and at least two strippers. Once I got into my thirties, it was slightly more sedate: moderate quantities of alcohol and just one stripper! Now that I'm in my late thirties, it would probably be a weekend walking with lots of good food.

Any advice for stag attendees?

Remember, it's about the groom-to-be, not everyone else. So the best man should respect his wishes and do what he wants. If that's something weird, like a *Deliverance*-style canoeing trip in the wilds in winter, or a visit to a taxidermy convention in France, so be it. It's the groom's call. Also, don't be afraid to stay sober, but if you do drink, don't ring home after six p.m.

What is uniquely British about the stag party?

How fixated we are with the alcohol aspect of it. In recent years, stag parties have gone from a night out in the local town or city to a full weekend, often overseas. But whatever else does or doesn't happen, booze is at the heart of it. People drink as much as they can, as quickly as they can. It's like a competition: first one to fall over wins—or maybe that should be *loses*!

THE PROFESSIONAL STAG DOER
Matthew B.

The trend of having larger, more extravagant prewedding celebrations seems universal. Matthew B., who owns Last Night of Freedom, a stag-planning company in the UK, told me a little bit about the history of the British ritual and his own experiences with the temptation to make the next stag "even bigger, better, faster, and harder."

I was reading an old book about how to run a stag night. It used to be that you could have only your unmarried friends. And the etiquette was that you went to a gentlemen's club, and you had some food and drinks and smoked cigars. And then your mates would do a couple of speeches for you. Then you might have a stripper or someone to come and dance for you, but it wouldn't be like what *we* know as a stripper or dancer. It would be more like light entertainment: A woman would turn up and maybe sing a song or something. And you were expected to leave by about eleven o'clock. That was back in the 1920s.

It always used to be a stag night, but now it's a stag *weekend*. Currently we do eleven hundred stag weekends a year. It's a sixty-forty split between the UK and going abroad. Everyone used to go to Dublin. But they sort of had a bit of a clampdown there. Dublin did a reasonably famous survey, and what they found was that for every pound they generated in stag income, something like two pounds were put off from coming, because of the stags. So they asked the hotels not to allow in single-sex parties of males over a certain number. And they wouldn't let in groups of male parties over three people into any of the clubs and pubs. They just made you feel unwelcome. Now they kind of want the trade back.

We went to Riga in Latvia. Something about a place where health and safety isn't at the forefront is interesting to me.

We were doing some calculations not long ago about how much it brings into the local economy. Let's say a flight out there is going to be an average of one hundred fifty pounds. Then you've got accommodations, so let's just say you pay eighty pounds for accommodations, and you do fifty pounds worth of activities. And you're probably going to spend somewhere in the region of one hundred twenty pounds on drinking. And then an additional fifty quid on incidentals: miscellaneous things and food. And that is for middle-of-the-range groups. You're looking at each person bringing about four hundred fifty quid. If you multiply that by the average group size of thirteen, each group brings that country 5,850 pounds, which is about eleven thousand dollars in the U.S.

With Eastern Europe opening up, everyone just went off

and had their stag weekends there instead of Dublin, or even Amsterdam. There are a lot of different reasons that going to Eastern Europe is attractive for a stag do: There has always been the fascination with communism, really. You never get to see it; it's forbidden fruit in a way. And it's got a reasonably glamorous side to it, as well as a nasty side. So there's a lot of intrigue. Also, I don't know if you have ever seen Eastern European women but, fucking hell, it's just disgusting how good-looking they are.

If the Berlin Wall hadn't come down, then we wouldn't be in business the way we are—that, combined with all the no-frills airlines that we've got over here. But to be quite honest, Prague's been ruined by stag weekends. I would say that hundreds of stag dos go there every weekend. And that is *not* something we really want to push. We do not want a place that is full of other stag groups. You don't mind the occasional one, but you want to feel like you're the guy on your weekend.

I got married pretty recently. Officially, my best man planned my stag, but really a lot of it was me. To be fair, I said I knew all the contacts and everything. I didn't have anything to do with the final details, but I kind of set it up because I knew what I wanted to do. And if you run a stag company, there's a little pressure to set the bar high.

We went to Riga in Latvia. I'd gone there a few years earlier and I just loved the place. It was unashamedly Eastern Block; it had all the charms of a place having its first flirtation with capitalism. Everything was fun and cool, and people weren't sick of the British. Everything was a novelty and everyone was just pleased not to be living in communism, basically. And something about a place where health and safety isn't at the forefront is interesting to me. It's just so different from what we've got in the sanitized, safe, nanny state of Britain. It's got a bit of an edge, a bit of life to it. And also, seriously, when you see the women over there, just to look at them is amazing. I think they must deport the bad-looking women or something.

Really what I wanted was for us all to enjoy a reasonably structured time without it being too in your face. When we got there, I wanted everyone to look around and actually have an appreciation for where we were, not just think of it as somewhere to get pissed[8]. I hate it when people don't really care where they go. I wanted everyone to know the history behind Latvia and a little bit about the people that we were going to be drinking with in the night.

I kind of got a sniff that my friends might be getting a strip limo, and I didn't do anything to stop it. A strip limo is just strippers in a limo, basically. They're totally nude and they'll touch you, but you can't touch them. You wouldn't, you know. . . . It's totally the wrong forum for that sort of thing anyway. This is more about titillation.

Then we went to a medieval restaurant and had medieval food brought to us. And we all passed around this hard-core liquor that they've got over there called Balsam. We drank massive amounts of it the rest of the night.

What made my stag different were the activities. None of us had really done any of those things before: No one had shot all

---

8 pissed (adj) *slang* British, drunk

the guns that we shot, and no one had been down a bobsled track before. No one had seen that many good-looking women in one place. And no one had ever been to Latvia, apart from me. I don't think we'll get that again on subsequent stags. I was the first of my mates to get married, so we got all that freshness. Eventually everything gets a bit clichéd.

So before you went on your stag, did you talk to your wife about it?

She didn't really want me to have any strippers, but I think she sort of knew that she was fighting a losing battle. Apart from that, she just sort of told me to behave. She was having her hen weekend[9] the weekend after, so her threat was that whatever I got into, she would too. Hen weekends are a massive thing over here as well; they're just as wild as the stag dos. It is not exactly equal now, but just about.

We also have coed parties called hag weekends. It's just such the lamest thing. I imagine the sort of person to do a hag weekend is someone who has lost all spirit to them. You do couples' weekends all the time, so I don't think there's any excuse for one just before you are married. I'm really sort of against the idea. I think it's important to keep the same-sex bonds, to be able to go out and just have your male friends. I'm not saying you have a better time with just the lads, but it doesn't happen so often these days. So

....

9 hen weekend the British (and Australian) equivalent of the bachelorette party weekend when you do get the opportunity, you need to grab hold of it with both hands.

Now all of the stag companies are competing for the most extreme stag weekend. We've sort of taken the mickey out of it a bit by offering to do one to the North Pole. It would be great, but it's probably not going to happen because it costs five thousand pounds ($9,350 U.S.) a person.

GOING GLOBAL INDIA

The Farewell Feast of the Five Bachelors sounds suspiciously like a bachelor party: an Indian groom-to-be eats dinner with his unmarried male friends to mark his last days of bachelorhood. But, unlike Western traditions, this bash includes activities that demonstrate the groom's commitment to his imminent marriage. After the meal, the men dig a hole and the groom sits over it. They pour water over him and collect it in a pitcher as it runs through his hair. Later he brings the pitcher to his lucky bride's house as a sign of his devotion.

THE COLOMBIAN BACHELOR
Alvaro N.

The British are increasingly socially mobile, with, for example, the queen bestowing royal titles upon rock stars like Sir Mick Jagger—regardless of his station at birth. Similarly, the

American Dream has always been fueled by the promise that one's potential need not be limited by one's background. But in many countries, like Colombia, the class you're born into is the class you remain in—generation after generation after generation. "There is a social wall between the classes," explains Alvaro N., who grew up in Bogotá firmly in the upper class. "But I don't agree with that anymore," adds the twenty-nine-year-old South American, who has lived in New York for almost five years. He recently returned to Colombia for the week leading up to his wedding, and the realities of social rank were pretty striking—especially during the bachelor party festivities.

They're called *despedida de solteiro* in Colombia, which translates to "farewell of the bachelor." When it came to my wedding, that was all my friends talked about. They said, "We're planning your party." It was not something where I could say, "No, I don't want it."

I haven't been to many bachelor parties, but I actually had two in Colombia. The first one was with my friends from college; the second one was with my friends from high school. I'm very close to both groups, and each one came up with the idea of throwing a bachelor party for me.

My high school was a higher class, and my college was a public college. One friend from high school says that he's going to be the president of Colombia, and I wouldn't doubt it. But my friends from the public college, they're not in my same class level. That might have been why I kept both groups separate—we do that a lot in Colombia.

The first party I got was from the guys from college. I don't know why, but with this college group there's always been a lack of girls. So for them, this bachelor party was a good excuse to have naked girls around. It was held at a friend's small apartment. He still lives with his mom, but he asked her to stay somewhere else during the bachelor party.

I got there and we drank some rum. Finally two girls came. They were young—I'm not saying they were underage—and both were very good-looking. They had costumes on: One girl was dressed as a nurse, and the other was dressed as a police girl.

These girls were hardcore. They were dancing to *reggeaton*[10] and did a lap dance for each person in the room—there were maybe nine guys. And the girls did what they call a lesbian show. They had brought dildos and they let themselves be touched by the people in the room, even during their show. There was no sex—I guess because of a lack of money—but these girls were ready for it.

The wedding was on Saturday. That party was Wednesday. Then comes Thursday and the party with my friends from high school. The whole thing started off at a pub. Since I had been living away, part of it was a welcome party. You know, "How's work? How are you?" I didn't want to talk about the party I'd had the day before. I don't know why: I just think they are separate groups and I keep them separate.

We had a couple of beers at the pub. After a while it was like, "Okay, we are ready to go." We got in two cabs. The place we

....

10 *reggeaton* a popular style of music that blends reggae, dancehall, and traditional Latin American rhythms with spoken-word rapping and a hip-hop sensibility went to is called La Forty-Nine. And this is—how do you say?—a whorehouse. There are girls walking in skimpy clothes everywhere. But the girls were not as nice as the ones from the night before, even though there were a lot more. I don't know how to describe it in a polite way, but these ones had the bitch look, the whore look; you look at them and you say, "I know what you do for a living."

A lot of these girls who work as strippers or prostitutes come from towns outside the city and from all over Colombia. And they get to Bogotá and have to face a tough reality of no jobs. Colombia is ultrareligious—it's Catholic—and I'm sure that most of these girls are Catholic. They probably go to mass and have figurines of saints. I don't know if they pray, "Tonight I hope I have clients," but I do think that they are firm believers and that they have to do this work. If they don't, they will die. It's sad, but that was not the moment to think about it.

So they take us to the second floor and it's just our group and one other table. We ordered rum. And the girls come. What they're trained to do is sit down at your table and drink your drinks; that way you have to buy more.

My friends start flirting with the girls. Then there's this one girl that's hanging around us. The thing is that my friends have paid her to dance for me. She dances, takes her clothes off, puts her legs on top of my shoulders—I guess the usual type of stuff. And then she starts to pressure me: "Do you want? Do you want?" And I think a lot of guys getting married say, "It's one last screw." But I had been living with my girlfriend for a couple of years, so it didn't seem like the right thing to do. I just said, "No, I'll pass."

And these girls weren't very appealing. What was a little

uncomfortable was that my friends were interested. There came a moment when I found myself sitting there with one of these girls, but none of my friends were there. They'd all gone off and left their jackets with me.

Maybe I did subconsciously think about the fact that these girls evidently come from a different socioeconomic background: I mean, you know your country and the different accents and where people are from. And a high-class girl would not be working at one of these brothels in Bogotá. Whereas I do feel that in New York, maybe your neighbor or the girl that's next to you on the subway might work at a strip club. And that changes your perspective. So maybe it did influence my decision to not actually have sex at my bachelor party—thinking that it's not very fair. I don't think that was an issue for my friends. It's just how everybody does things there.

GOING GLOBAL
MOROCCO

The groom, who spends the night treated like—and dressed as—a sultan, is followed by his "court," who fire gunshots while they parade through the streets. Traditionally the women gather for their own prewedding festivities, where the *schikhatt* is staged. It is an erotic dance performed by a *sheikha* (translation: "wise, older woman") and her all-female group of musicians and dancers. The purpose is to educate the presumed virginal bride on how she will be expected to move in the marriage bed.

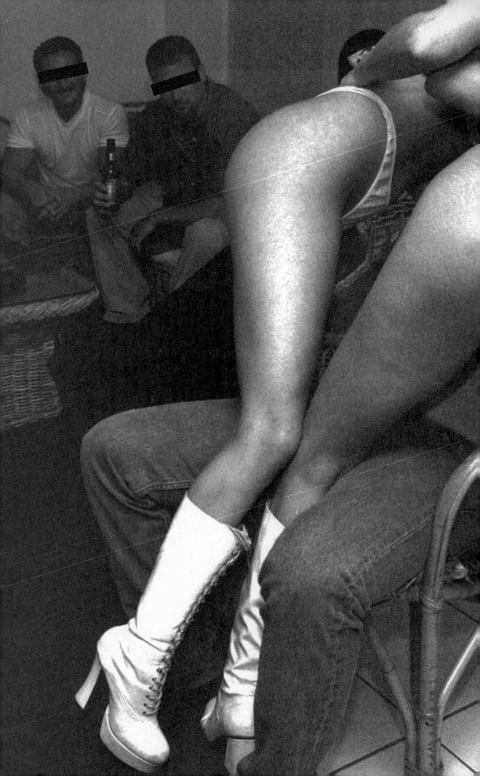

Chapter 8

Welcome to the Jungle

FROM THAT VERY FIRST BACHELOR PARTY I attended—my cousin's, almost twenty years ago—I wondered what was fueling this extreme mode of partying and why it was a required leg in the wedding marathon.

It varies from person to person, but this ritual clearly connects men to our animalistic, primitive roots. Granted, instead of hunting prey and kidnapping brides, guys like my cousin smoke pot and hire strippers. And instead of feats of strength and mortal combat, my cousin's pack determined who was top dog by seeing who could drink the most beers and pick up the hottest women.

Is this what survival of the fittest has come to? If so, I know one guy whose genes are likely to survive.

THE PARTY ANIMAL
Anthony V.

Unfiltered and unabashed, Anthony V. provided a rare and candid glimpse of the more animalistic nature of men and their ritual. Arguably, he is closer to man's primal roots than most. "Honestly, I just love to fucking fuck women." The thirty-three-year-old businessman believes that, left to their own devices in a world without snitches, alimony, and the stigma of adultery, most men would have sex with women other than their wives.

A great storyteller with a filthy, filthy mouth, he eased any lingering doubts that I was collecting mostly PG-13 versions of a presumably X-rated ritual. Even he realized that some might find his tone and beliefs a little shocking. "I know I may sound like a prick," he admitted, "but I am being really honest." So consider yourself warned.

I'd probably say I've been to about a half dozen bachelor parties. One was so good that it's probably one of the best days of my life. It was in 1996.

Basically here's how it started off: We were waiting and waiting for this bus to pick us all up to take us to a steakhouse. And we're waiting and fuckin' waiting and fuckin' waiting and nothing. All of a sudden, out of nowhere, we see this really tall guy walking toward a limousine that pulled up right in front of us. I turn around and go, "Oh, shit, it's Howard Stern." He waves to us, gets into the limo, and drives off. And I'm like, "Okay, that was a good omen." Two minutes later, the bus pulls up and we get in. There's porn playing. Guys are smoking pot and some are doin' coke.

We go to the restaurant. I don't even know how much the fucking bill was, but we had the entire upstairs. It was like twenty of us, eating probably a half a cow each. Then they started bringing other people in. I felt so bad for them, to have to spend so much money on a meal in a room filled with screaming and ranting from a bunch of drunken, stoned morons.

And that was just the beginning. We had a suite at a Marriot, but before we go there, we went to a strip club nearby and spent a few hours, blowin' money on strippers and booze and hanging out. Then we go back to the hotel. And these two chicks show up to do a show for us. It was fucking unbelievable. This one chick was Russian, the other girl was British. A blonde and a brunette. And they're doin' this show where this one chick puts a piece of banana inside of her cunt and shoots it into the mouth of the other girl. So we're all sitting around in this circle watching this shit, and one of the girls says, "Okay, does anybody want to spit in my pussy?" My friend gets up and says, "I'll do it." And he goes and spits in this chick's pussy, and starts to like lube her up. And we're all just screaming.

Now there's only one black guy in the entire party. We were calling him O.J. the entire night—this was the mid nineties. It was all in good nature, you know? It wasn't like we were trying to put him down. Anyway, the strippers say, "We need somebody over here to pull out their cock." So this motherfucker gets up. And you know the myth of black guys being really huge? Well that fuckin' myth became a reality that night. Every fucking white guy in that room, our jaws dropped. And this guy went from being called O.J. to being called the Boomerang, because he had this giant fuckin' cock that was curved to the left—big-time. Here I am, I'm Italian and I'm thinkin' I've got a pretty good-size cock, and I was just nothing compared to this guy. I don't even know what the strippers did with him, but it was just beyond hysterical.

So the party continues. Everybody's smokin', drinking, eating. All of a sudden, we turn around and one of my friends—a real old-school, fat, Italian-type guy—is in the middle of the fucking living room with his pants around his fuckin' ankles and his hands are on his waist, like how Superman would stand—you know, showing off his chest. And he's getting blown by one of the two women. So we all start screaming, "Hey, it's fucking Superman getting blown."

Infamous Bachelor Parties:
BEN AFFLECK, 2003 (CANCELED)

After photos of Affleck cavorting with strippers in a Canadian club surfaced, fiancé **J. Lo** allegedly demanded that Affleck cancel his bachelor party on Hooter's Air that was being planned by his brother, Casey. That **Bennifer** wedding was eventually called off. But in 2005 Affleck kept the Bennifer family name alive, marrying **Jennifer Garner** after a low-key bachelor party at the couple's Brentwood home.

I'm kinda the stud at this time and I decide, "You know what? I want both of these broads." So I take 'em into the bathroom. And I'm gettin' blown by both of them, and fuckin' around. All of a sudden, my friend creeps into the bathroom, and he's so shit-faced that he doesn't even know what he's sayin', and he's just watching me getting blown. I'm like, "What are you doin' here, man? Get the fuck outta here." And he's just rambling on—nothing coherent. He tries to leave and the door creaks open, and, literally, it looked like a *Little Rascals* TV show, where one head on top of the other pops in to look inside the room. And there's eight guys watching me get fuckin' blown. I'm like, "Guys! Come on—give me a little privacy here!"

Believe it or not, that's how I met my ex-wife. She was one of the strippers —at a fake bachelor party— and I was the "bachelor."

Then this other stripper shows up. This really big blonde with big, fake fuckin' tits. And there's a bedroom in this suite; I guess that's obvious. Boomerang was actually fucking this whore—without a fuckin' condom—in the middle of the fuckin' bedroom. We're all like, "Oh my God!" And he's giving it to her balls fuckin' deep. And we're just falling about the place losing our fuckin' minds. I'm lookin' at this and I'm like, "Oh my God, this is like watching a fuckin' porno." So I walk into the bedroom and sit down on the floor. And I pull my dick out and start jerkin' off. And this fuckin' whore lifts her head, sees me, and she's like, "Hey, you can't do that. That's gonna cost you fifty bucks." And I'm like, "Fuck you!" Another guy walks in and he's lookin' at this guy fuckin' this broad on the bed, and he sees me there whackin' off, and he shrugs his shoulders and goes, "Oh, okay." He goes to the other side of the room and he does the same thing. The two of us are just sittin' there, jerkin' off to live porn.

I'm missing some details, but that's probably one of the funniest nights of my life. It just was ridiculously cool. The bachelor didn't do a thing though; he was really good. I swear to God. He's divorced now, so I could say whatever I want. But he was really good.

Infamous Bachelor Parties:
MARIO LOPEZ, 2004

The actor best known for his portrayal of Slater on *Saved by the Bell* allegedly cheated on his bride-to-be, former Miss Teen USA **Ali Landry**, at his bachelor party in Acapulco. The C-list couple went on with their nuptials and allowed Oprah Winfrey's crew to film the whole thing for a never-to-be-aired segment. Two weeks later, Landry filed for an annulment.

Now, what's really interesting—fast forward to a bunch of friends who would get together and throw fake bachelor parties. One of us would be the bachelor for the night. And they'd hire a bunch of girls to come over to do a show. Most of these guys were married and one of them was a doctor; he'd bring the latex gloves for everybody so that they could touch and finger the girls and, like, somehow rationalize in their minds that they weren't cheating on their wives.

Believe it or not, that's how I met my ex-wife. She was one of the strippers for the night—at a *fake* bachelor party—and I was the "bachelor." She was at this party and she looked really hot. And they did this show in which they actually—I don't know how they do it—but they were able to put the front of a guy's foot inside their vaginas. It was pretty gross, but it was fun.

After the show I take these two chicks upstairs. I fuck one of them and she leaves. I start fucking the other one, and we have this amazing time. We actually were making out; usually whores don't make out with you. And I'm just smitten with this girl, so I slipped her a note. Afterward I said, "Hey, would you like me to give you a ride home?" And she's like, "Aren't you getting married?" I said, "No, you know . . ." And I told her the whole story. She invited me up to her place and I spent the next three days there. Somehow I managed to fall in love with this chick and ended up wasting eight years of my life with her.

It was a very tumultuous relationship. She was very troubled; she had a very rough life. Her self-worth was horrible. But the sweet guy I am, I decided I was going to try anyway. And I tried and tried and tried, and ended up marrying her.

So, did you have a bachelor party?

No. Because of her background, she was freaking out about that. I had to change so many things about my life and my lifestyle to make her feel more secure. I didn't even have a bachelor party. Instead I went to dinner with a bunch of friends and went out to a bar. And she showed up there, all fucked up in the head, and just freaking out about marrying me and this and that. I'm just going, "What the fuck is she doing here?" There are so many fucking telltale signs. My friend reminded me about seven months ago, after I got divorced, that before I got married, I said, "I am going to try to make this work for a few years, and if I can't, I'm out."

I tried very hard. That is just how I was brought up: If you get married, you try to make it work. Eventually I got her to quit stripping, but I couldn't get her to get a job, and it started getting really frustrating. I just didn't feel like I had a partner—a person who was in it with me to try to build a future. And I wasn't appreciated for all the contributions I was making to our relationship. I felt like I was in it alone. So, after a certain point, I said, "There are only so many years that I can be a complete sucker." That's how I felt—so pissed off and fed up.

I missed so many of my friends' bachelor parties to make that fucking bitch happy. I swore after I got divorced that I would have a real bachelor party. I just got a killer apartment, so I've got to get my friends together and throw the bachelor party of all bachelor parties. And it's a bachelor party, in the sense that I've become a bachelor again. I want a fuckin' Great Dane fucking some black chick balls deep on a fuckin' card table during Texas Hold 'Em. I want this to be fucking crazy. You've gotten me thinking about it, and we're going to have to set this up.

Believe it or not, I could see myself being married again, but I could not see myself being monogamous. If I were to get married, I would just have to tell her, "Look, monogamy is just not in my blood." I realize that now, because I was faithful in my marriage. But we have been fed such a line of bullshit about what love is. We're taught that if you love somebody, you are with them and only them. You know what, man? I could fuck a dozen women and still love the woman I'm with.

Infamous Bachelor Parties:
PARIS LASTIS, 2005

Instant replay: **Paris Hilton** dumped her fiancé Paris Lastis after learning that the Greek shipping heir cheated on her at his bachelor party. In a televised interview with *Extra*, she advised all grooms-to-be, "Don't cheat on her at your bachelor party. It's gross what you guys do at those parties. Whoever I marry is not going to have a bachelor party."

THE DOMESTICATED GROOM
Chris S.

Thirty-six-year-old army veteran Chris S. used to be a lot like Anthony, but he's changed. For Chris, who took a platoon into Kosovo and now lives in Georgia, his bachelor party was more of an obligation than a last night of freedom.

I raised hell before I met my wife. I had lots of different women and would sleep with several different ones in a day. Then I fell in love with my wife and fell out of that craziness. Some people will party like a rock star until the very end, but some of us fall in love and we don't care to chase pussy—especially right before marriage.

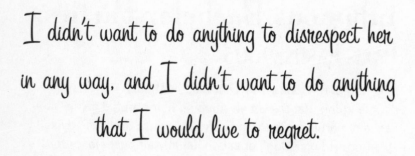

I didn't want to do anything to disrespect her in any way, and I didn't want to do anything that I would live to regret.

My wife left the bachelor party up to me; she knew I would do whatever I wanted to do anyway. But she did tell me that she hoped that I wouldn't do things with strippers. I'm sure she thought I would, because she's heard about other bachelor parties I had been to, some really crazy ones with women doing each other with bananas, doing group shows, and shit like that.

But I didn't want to do anything to disrespect her in any way, and I didn't want to do anything that I would live to regret.

My bachelor party was kind of low-key. We went out, just a bunch of my friends, to a bar where my brother's a regular and got as drunk as we possibly could. My best man set it up. I gave him a little bit of instructions. I told him I wasn't into the kinky shit. Other than that, I didn't care what happened.

If you don't have one, your friends feel short-changed. And some of the people that would have come to the bachelor party didn't because they knew that I wasn't going to go crazy. But that's all right—to each his own.

Lessons from Guyville

"*YOU'RE* THE GUY WRITING THE BACHELOR PARTY book? I was expecting someone more like a marine." Those were the first words out of the publisher's mouth when we were introduced. Maybe not a vote of confidence, but totally understandable.

I am *not* the obvious choice to write this book. But consider this: Closeted until after college, I've spent plenty of time doing my best impersonation of a straight dude. I've been to more than two dozen weddings. And hetero friends continue to seek my counsel when it comes to matters of love and lust. In other words, some of my best friends are straight.

But, as a gay man working on a book about bachelor parties, I quickly recognized that I was a tourist in Guyville. During one of the first interviews, I naively asked Andy W.,

"What's the deal with vaginas? What's the attraction?" He was speechless, then said, "I'm not going to answer that." I could sense suspicions creeping in and my status shifting from part-ner-in-crime to enemy combatant.

From then on, I tried my best to blend in. In a sense, I went back into the closet to get the story: I did most interviews by phone. I avoided even remotely homoerotic questions. And when participants inquired about my marital status, I dodged the truth—sometimes I outright lied. I can't say I feel good about that, but I know the book is truer for it.

Let's face it: Most guys probably prefer this book never see the light of day. They have a pretty good scam going. The bache-lor party has become their get-out-of-jail-free pass that women have a hard time refusing. If I were in their shoes, I wouldn't want to jeopardize it, either, and I wouldn't fully trust an out-sider to tell my story.

That it's gotten to this point—with men needing to use the rite as excuse to gather—should raise a red flag about the demands of modern relationships and the needs of modern men. That the traditional night before has been transformed into a weeklong pleasure binge suggests that men are making a conscious decision to make the most of their time away from their significant others.

Sure, a few will use that time to bang a stripper, but most will simply choose to let their hair down. Free from the role of spouse, parent, boss, citizen, they'll boast about exploits and trash talk with impunity. It may seem mundane and soulless, but for some this is all they have. Or as Felix C. pointed out,

"If you don't do weekends like this, then what the fuck's the point?"

I hope the men I interviewed feel heard and represented. I've tried my best to be fair while making my way through their smoke screens. (Maybe you noticed that not a single participant admitted to cheating on his partner—it's always a friend or, better still, an acquaintance.)

Most of the women I spoke with told me they wanted to know "what really goes on." I've done my best to deliver that, too. Some passages may be shocking, but probably nothing worse than you imagined. And if there's one thing I've realized, no matter what I say, most of you will continue to believe your man is different. Maybe he is. But, for argument's sake, let's say that he does check out other women once in a while and that, given immunity, some men might even have sex with a supermodel or, more realistically, a prostitute. None of this means he loves you any less. In fact it doesn't really have much to do with *you*. Sometimes he thinks with his dick, not his heart.

But nervous brides-to-be should take comfort: Your beloved is probably not going to stray too far at his bachelor party. According to stripper June T., "It usually is *not* the bachelor asking for extras, because he is still in a state of romance, he is still holding on to the ideal." The bad news, as June notes—and pretty much every stripper confirmed—is, "The ones who try to slip their hand right to the edge of your G-string or to the bottom of your breast are always the ones with a wedding ring on." That, like much of what I learned during my two-year odyssey, surprised me, too.

So what *is* my take on the ritual? At its best, a bachelor party allows friends to celebrate what's unique about the groom and promises that rare opportunity for unmitigated, uninterrupted male bonding. At its worst, it's a spoonful of dirty that makes the wedding go down and a ready-made excuse to push the envelope. We can certainly hope their better angels prevail, but maybe it's okay even when they don't.

WHAT DO YOU THINK?

Share your stories and opinions at
www.bachelorparties.org
or
www.myspace.com/bachelorparties

Photo Credits

Introduction: Why Me?
Sam Menchyk

Ch 1: He Said, She Said
Tomas Hellberg

Ch 2: The More Things Change, the More They Stay the Same
From the documentary *The Bronx Boys*

Ch 3: That's Entertainment!
Colby Katz

Ch 4: What Happens in Vegas . . .
Declan Durcan

Ch 5: And Now for Something Completely Different
Tomas Hellberg

Ch 6: We Have a Situation
Anonymous

Ch 7: It's a Small World After All
Chris Cho

Ch 8: Welcome to the Jungle
Colby Katz

Epilogue: Lessons from Guyville
Michael C. Kudriavtseff

Author photo:
Sam Zalutsky

Acknowledgements

First, thanks to the brave souls who shared their stories; I hope I did them justice and that you dig *Bachelor Party Confidential*.

This book would never have come together without the folks who read various drafts and offered insightful feedback every step of the way, including Liz Donahue, Abby Ellin, John Garrison, Doni Gewirtzman, Piper Kerman, Robert Levy, Dan Sacher, Larry Smith, David Thorpe, and Penelope Whitney.

Thanks to everyone who helped me find interesting people with interesting stories, (to protect identities of participants, I'll stick to first names and last initials of their recruiters): Fay and Stu B., Amy G., Judy G., Vestal M., Jane P., Colleen W., Liz S., Rachel G., Tom D., Matt S., Sandi D., Jimz N., Kerry K., Brad G., Elliot K., Kelly M., Danny X., Matt S., Kaethe F., Ellen G., Adam G., Lisa H., Ivy C., Steffan S., Mimi O., Annabrooke T., Versed, Pigmalions, and all the rest of you who forwarded an email or nagged family and friends on my behalf. Thanks also to transcribing superstars Kerri Wood and Esinam Bediako (also a great researcher), as well as researcher Madeleine Gran.

A few final shout-outs to those near and dear who've listened to me talk about bachelor parties for the better part of two years and offered encouraging words and general enthusiasm: Kim McGalliard (with whom it all began), Elana Koff, Alberto Orso, Sam Zalutsky (who also took that dashing author photo), Ed Boland, Jeff Lee, Ted & Molly, Candy & Toad, David Mills, Trent Hanover, Ellen Umansky, my travelmates Lenny & Craig, publicity dynamo Jessica Krakoski, Gorilla Coffee, Ken Helman and the whole Boyer clan. And, of course, my unending gratitude to the lovely and talented (and patient) Patrick Price and the talented and lovely (and visionary) Trish Boczkowski.